GEORG TRAKL : A

GEORG TRAKL

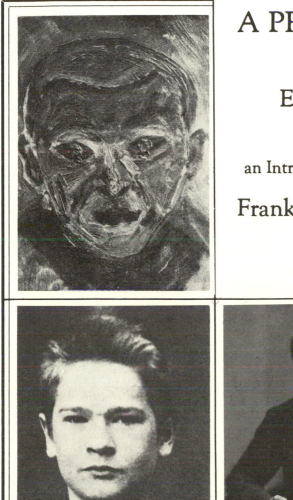

A PROFILE

Edited,

with
an Introduction, by

Frank Graziano

LOGBRIDGE-RHODES

Grateful acknowledgement is extended to the Austrian Institute in New York City for assistance which helped make this volume a possibility. Sincere thanks are also due to the estate of Georg Trakl, Otto Müller Verlag, Jonathan Cape Ltd., Anne Wright, Wesleyan University Press, and the translators. First publication citations and details regarding translation rights may be found on the last printed pages of this book, which constitute a continuation of the copyright notices below.

The title pages of this edition are illustrated with photographs of Georg Trakl at various ages; of Trakl's self-portrait; of Trakl's sister Grete (prose poem title page); and of Trakl's mother, father and friend Erhard Buschbeck (letters title page). All photographs were supplied by and reprinted with the permission of the Otto Müller Verlag in Salzburg.

Library of Congress Cataloging-in-Publication data may be found on the last printed page of this book.

This is the first edition.

Printed in the United States of America for:

Logbridge-Rhodes, Inc.
Post Office Box 3254
Durango, Colorado 81301

CONTENTS

Who could he have been?

—Rainer Maria Rilke
on Georg Trakl

INTRODUCTION

Frank Graziano

And one always is thrown back upon words or,
better expressed, upon terrible helplessness.
                                        —Trakl

Harold Bloom has reminded us of the etymological relationship
between "meaning" and "moaning"; "a poem's meaning," he
argued, "is a poem's complaint." "Complaint," however, misses
the mark when dealing with a poem by Georg Trakl; it suits only
poets whose work gives priority to what a word *says* over what a
word *is*, to the chatter of signification over the fullness of diction
not dependent primarily upon meaning. Anne Sexton complains,
Georg Trakl does nothing short of moan. Meticulous listeners
know that it is precisely a fundamental *lack*, a nucleus of absence
often signalled by the break in the tone of a moaner's voice, that
endows a moan with emotional impact, with meaning. When the
bottom falls out of a voice we listen, we attend quickly to what-is-
missing. Kojève has quite deftly defined desire as the presence of
an absence; moans (be they voiced or poetic) are the intonation of
that presence. We are enticed by the béance of moans and thus
engage in the plea their longing wagers, in their desire—as Hegel
would have it—to make their desire recognized. The moaner, like
the analysand, like Trakl, enjoys a degree of relief and gratifi-
cation merely by making his private gloom public, by objectifying
the antithesis of his lack and drawing the listener inside it. Any
moan, until it runs out of breath, grants reprieve from a painful
silence, "The silence of decayed crosses on the hill." The moans
most meticulously formalized into poems, ironically, seem almost
to breathe back into their own hollows—to engender their own *in-
spiration* and sustenance—and thus long survive the author they
failed.

One can devour a doughnut, Osip Mandelstam once said out of
the side of his mouth, but the hole will remain. Trakl criticism has
devoured the doughnut. Georg Trakl was a poetic genius precisely
because he was insane enough to unwittingly author texts too
elusive to accommodate systematic exegeses or compact formulae,
texts that, more than anything, attempt to rectify the absence that
bore them and that therefore are best defined, like doughnuts, by
what they lack. Trakl's canon, borrowing a phrase Anthony
Wilder used summarizing Lacan, "is as dependent upon the notion
of lack as is the theory of desire." It was Rilke who first realized

that Trakl built his poems on pauses, on the moments when help-lessness made the unmoaned lack seem enough, when the poem almost went unwritten. One can imagine Trakl's brief, intoxicated life as one that mortifies its flesh only to patch it with poems bear-ing an uncanny semblance to scars, poems which were, as Trakl put it, imperfect penance. The penitent and poet-as-penitent beg pardon from a silent god who bestows grace only upon those who convince themselves that a deity is listening; it is the *assumption* of audience that affords a measure of absolution. Those who knew Trakl personally tell us that he was—as one might expect after reading his poems—frequently inaccessible and obscure, that in-stead of engaging in conversation he was inclined to monologue strangely to an audience he needed but could not quite face, his gaze cocked into the distance. Trakl was even known to pay a dilapidated whore her fee to hear out his oracular harangues. Whether or not this prostitute understood him, whether or not the presumed god hears and acknowledges the prayer, whether or not the reader of the following poems decodes Trakl's "meaning" is, for all practical purposes, quite beside the point. While Trakl's poem-monologues have, due to their affinity with moans, been spared the bombast of his oral soliloquies, they do follow the suit of these cryptic speechifications (and of the silent discourse of the deities) by refusing the passive reader with conventional strategies any dialogue or dialectic, any access. Requisite for appreciation of these poems is a sensitivity to the lack Trakl spoke from, to their desire for an audience and their simultaneous inability to face it, and to the resulting but paradoxical fact that density was a necessary condition of their composition and not an overcoat im-posed for the joy of obfuscation. Trakl's poems invite the reader in, one might say, but never ask that he make himself at home. "I do not understand them," Ludwig Wittgenstein wrote after anonymously granting Trakl twenty thousand Austrian crowns, "but their tone delights me. It is the tone of a man of real genius."

Meaning in the Trakl poem, then, as in the penance prayer, is most often secondary to doing. Trakl's fidelity was to the tone he generated by carrying often-synaesthetic images on rhythms whose syntax now and then strategically—but necessarily—collapsed, necessarily because the world order imposed and enforced by grammar was untrue to this poet's experience. Trakl gave his pre-articulate gloom to "the living fever" and "an infernal chaos of rhythms and images" in order to rid himself of or lose himself in the structure of tonally powerful constructs, in moans that gained a measure of meaning almost incidentally from the language that gave them form. Trakl was speaking to himself when, in his 1908

10

review of a neo-Romantic drama, he said:

> In these lines there is something of the sweet, feminine
> rhetoric which seduces us to listen to the melos of the
> word and to ignore its content and significance.

Michael Hamburger's phrase "strangely quiet and pure" would
well replace the passage's "sweet" and "feminine" if we were to
have this quotation address Trakl's work specifically, but in any
case our author here offers a route into his hermetic and difficult
texts: willingness to be lolled along and seduced by the beautiful
gloom of language not dominated by meaning, willingness, one
might say, to ride the synthesis of rhythm and Angst. One must approach Trakl's discourse the way he, the reader, would approach
the discourse of madness: the manifest "meaning" of each text lies
not so much in what it says but rather in what it cleverly fails to
say, in what—by means of this failure and its inflections—it at
once conceals and suggests. A prominent suggestion in discourse
as such frequently presents itself in the form of an invitation—even
a plea—to undo the mast-text, the facade, and to hear the true
horror of the psychodynamics that launched it. That is the trap.
Readers of Trakl who attempt to accommodate this suggestion
eventually discover not only that every word—in Nietzsche's
metaphor—is a mask, but also that each of these masks has
nothing beneath it. While an analyst has his analysand's new texts
to inform a rendition of what-was-said and to dismantle the mask
and ultimately deliver the true intent of a particular discourse (or
symptom), the reader of Trakl has little more than the original
word—the poem itself—and thus has no reasonable alternative
but to direct his attention to activity dealing not with disclosing
the secret significance or the latent enterprise of truth in Trakl's
poems, but rather with the virtue of the arational and the dark
lost-on-earthness that each Trakl poem exacts through tonal, im-
agistic and sonic density. The task is not to "cure" the poem or its
dead author by unearthing the hidden agenda, of course, but
rather to experience the interaction of psychopathology and
aesthetics and the unique vision—the unique poetry—it affords.
To read Trakl is to be lost in and with him; to demand that one
conclusively orient himself in these texts and then discover an in-
tention never fully realized by the author himself merits an
honorable mention, again paraphrasing Lacan, for the art of
drawing the ultimate logical conclusion of an original misunder-
standing. Entering Trakl's canon is like entering a dark, abandoned cathedral after a promised ascension failed to occur. All of

the angels have already been extinguished. One is drawn into the moan when he succumbs to this sullen seduction, and here echoes a strangely beautiful, innocent voice still half buried in the ineffable.

II

Georg Trakl was born in Salzburg on February 3, 1887, and died twenty-seven years later from a self-induced overdose of cocaine. His father, Tobias Trakl, was Protestant both in faith and temperament, and was the proprietor of a thriving hardware store. After the death of his first wife, Tobias impregnated and subsequently married Maria Trakl, Georg's mother, who was fifteen years his junior. Maria was a married Catholic at the time of this impregnation, and thus divorced her first husband and converted to the Protestant church in preparation for life with Tobias. She was depressed and addicted to opium while the industrious Tobias thrived, but the couple shared common ground in indifference to their six children. Georg was the fourth, and he suffered the consequences of Maria's obsession with antiques and of Tobias' preoccupation with the business that afforded the affluent facade concealing this hotbed of insanity. Georg's younger sister Grete—a brilliant pianist and "the most beautiful girl, the greatest artist, the most unusual woman" as well as, if we accept the suggestion of both textual and extra-textual evidence, Georg's incestuous lover—was reared under his influence and resembled him strikingly in both appearance and psychopathology.

Trakl's youth was punctuated by a number of eerie events quite congruous with the tenor of his poetry. Some time between the ages of five and eight, for example, he walked directly into a pond until the cold water covered him over, his hat left floating on the surface. On another occasion he "cast himself down where black horses raced"; on another he attempted to throw himself in front of a moving train; and on another, years later, after having consumed an abundance of drugs, was found unconscious in the snow on a Salzburg hillside. Trakl also reported to friends that he never saw people's faces and had no notion of their physiognomy, and that until the age of twenty he saw nothing in his environment except water. "He did not believe that his father was his own," a physician later reported, "but rather imagined, that he descends from a cardinal and that in the future, he will become a great man." The same physician also noted that Trakl suffered from persecutory visual hallucinations, and that "he often hears bells ringing."

With the foundation of derangement suggested by these thoughts and acts Georg, at the age of ten, enrolled in an eight-year humanities program emphasizing Greek and Latin. His indifference to studies and his subsequent failure, his inclination to a pocketed flask of chloroform and cigarettes dipped in opium, and his disdain for the disciplinary ambience of his school caused him to disenroll during his seventh year.

Trakl's literary interests were always extra-academic. Between 1904 and 1906 he was a member of a writing club called "Apollo" (later changed to "Minerva"), and was appropriately Bohemian in dress and behavior. Having learned French as a child from an Alsatian governess, a censorious Catholic who sought to reform the "wayward" Trakl children, Georg read Baudelaire and Verlaine as well as a host of German-language poets, and held Nietzsche and Dostoevsky in the highest esteem. His earliest works were written—or overwritten—for the Apollo group, many of them prose poems in a rhetoric of passion and penance haunted by the strangeness of its author. Beginning in 1906 Trakl published prose and book reviews in a Salzburg newspaper, and at this time also authored two plays—*All Souls' Day* and *Fata Morgana*—both of which he destroyed after the second's poor critical reception. Trakl's emotional instability was apparent during the Apollo years, and his hints at suicide were frequent.

In September of 1905 Trakl became an apprentice in a Salzburg pharmacy, the White Angel. His course of study now called for a three-year apprenticeship which would fulfill the requirements for entry into a subsequent two-year program in pharmacy at the University of Vienna. The *poète maudit* had chosen a career that well suited his needs: the lover of drugs as pharmacist.

Studies commenced at the University of Vienna in the fall of 1908, and gloom overwhelmed Trakl. He moved from one furnished room to another, from one bar to the next during "days of ravening drunkenness and criminal melancholy...." His salvation was in Grete, who spent the year of 1909-1910 in Vienna studying music, and in Erhard Buschbeck, also of Salzburg, who commenced studies of law at the University in 1909. Buschbeck worked selflessly to introduce the pathologically bashful Trakl into literary circles, and to find publication outlets for his work. Trakl was largely beyond whatever hope Buschbeck had to offer, however, and in 1910, shortly before he took his degree, Trakl found his psychological desperation compounded by a financial one triggered by his father's death. When Tobias Trakl died the hardware store eventually died with him, and Trakl's source of financial security dissipated. Trakl's poverty reached its symbolic apex when the Bohemian poet, in all desperation for the quantities of drugs and alcohol to which he was accustomed, sold his prized collected works of Dostoevsky.

Immediately following his graduation Trakl was drafted into the Austrian army for a one-year term of duty. His education and middle-class status afforded him a relatively comfortable military existence, and the regimentation of military life may even have contributed positively to his emotional stability. Trakl, in any case, broke down after his discharge, roaming between various jobs in Vienna, Salzburg and Innsbruck. Confronted with the demands of his financial independence he attempted to reassume his old position at the White Angel, but was simply unable to cope with exposure to the pharmacy's customers, with the demands of human interaction. After a number of similar failures—jobs held for only a few hours or days—Trakl, in dire financial straits, re-enlisted into the army. He was assigned to the pharmacy of an Innsbruck military hospital in April of 1912.

Innsbruck proved fortunate for Trakl, for through the continued efforts of Buschbeck he was introduced to a circle of writers and intellectuals who recognized and fostered his talents. This group centered around the influential journal *Der Brenner*, which was edited by Ludwig von Ficker. After *Der Brenner* published its first piece by Trakl, Buschbeck, in May of 1912, arranged a meeting of poet and editor at Innsbruck's Cafe Maximilian. Ficker quickly became Trakl's guardian and patron as well as his friend, and was largely responsible for whatever security—personal as well as poetic—Trakl enjoyed in the remaining two years of his life. Trakl's best poems, "Helian" among them, were written under Ficker's influence, and no issue of *Der Brenner* between October 1912 and July 1914 appeared without Trakl's contribution.

As a result of exposure in *Der Brenner* Trakl was contacted by the poet and playwright Franz Werfel, a reader for the Kurt Wolff publishing house in Leipzig. Werfel requested a cohesive collection for publication in book form, and after a brief bout mediated by Ficker Trakl's first volume, *Gedichte (Poems)*, appeared in July of 1913. Arrangements were also made for a second volume, *Sebastian im Traum (Sebastian in Dream)*, which was issued posthumously in 1915.

In the summer of 1913 Trakl, having left active service, travelled to Venice with Karl Kraus, Adolf Loos, Peter Altenberg and Ficker. After a two-week vacation he returned to Vienna and, in November of 1913, to Innsbruck; these months, along with the first few months of 1914, were the most productive of his life.

Trakl's work was liberated under the influence of Rimbaud in 1912, and now, in this final period of productivity, was intensified by readings of Hölderlin.

A serious blow jeopardized whatever mental health Trakl maintained under Ficker's umbrella when, in March of 1914, Grete became seriously ill as the result of a miscarriage. Trakl rushed to Berlin and Grete's bedside. Grete was living through an unhappy marriage with Arthur Langen, a Berliner considerably her senior, and was depressed and addicted to drugs. Through Grete, who was active in Berlin's literary Bohemia, Trakl was introduced to one of the few women with whom he was able to relate, the poet Else Lasker-Schuler. (Trakl later dedicated one of his most important works, "Occident," to Lasker-Schuler.) Grete survived her illness of 1914, but less than three years later, after the suicide of her brother, she shot herself while attending a party.

In July of 1914 the philosopher Ludwig Wittgenstein donated a percentage of his patrimony for distribution to worthy Austrian writers at Ludwig von Ficker's discretion. Ficker allotted twenty thousand Austrian crowns each to both Trakl and Rilke, but the former's grant came too late to be of significant assistance. Trakl was so overcome with anxiety when he went to the bank with Ficker to withdraw his allotment that he ran from the building soaked in his own perspiration. Shortly after, when Austria declared war on Serbia on July 28, Trakl volunteered for active service and left Innsbruck, in August, with a field hospital unit destined for Galicia in Austria-occupied Poland. He never returned.

After the gruesome battle of Grodek (from which Trakl's last poem takes its title), Trakl was placed in charge of ninety serious casualties without the expertise or pharmaceuticals to treat them effectively. At one point the moans and agony cries of the injured soldiers were shattered by a gunshot; one suffering patient had committed suicide. Having run to attend to this death, Trakl was repulsed and overwhelmed by fragments of the patient's brain sticking to the wall. He ran from the barn in which the hospital was housed in order to escape this horror, but outside yet another nightmare awaited him: the limp bodies of hanged partisans were swinging from trees.

A few days later, during the disorganized retreat, Trakl stood up at dinner and announced that he could no longer live. Shortly after the attempted suicide that followed this announcement he was sent to the garrison hospital in Cracow for psychiatric observation. On November 3, 1914, after a visit from Ficker, Trakl overdosed on cocaine. Wittgenstein arrived three days after the poet's death in

15

response to a letter requesting his visit. Trakl was buried in Cracow, but in 1925 his remains were disinterred and moved to a cemetery near Ficker's home in Innsbruck.

III

With the 1975 release of Werner Herzog's *Every Man for Himself and God Against All* the Caspar Hauser legend, a legend that informs Trakl's poetry as much as his own biography, re-emerged with all the splendor of its strangeness. Hauser himself mysteriously appeared in a Nuremberg square on Whit-Monday, 1828, almost sixty years before Trakl's birth. He had been secured since birth to the floor of an underground dungeon which, as Herzog aptly states it, "he apparently accepts as a part of his anatomy." After sixteen or seventeen years of imprisonment Hauser was suddenly released by his jailer. When he was discovered in Nuremberg he could hardly walk or speak (his single sentence reportedly being "I want to be a horseman"), and would only take bread and water. Caspar Hauser eventually became a ward of the city and was educated under the direction of Ritter Anselm von Feuerbach (the philosopher's father) until, in 1883, he was attacked and stabbed to death by an unknown assailant. His death, to this day, remains as mysterious as his appearance.

While Georg Trakl's interest in Caspar Hauser may appear at first glance to be no more than literary (Trakl modelled his "Caspar Hauser Song" on Verlaine's poem by the same title, and on Jacob Wassermann's novel *Caspar Hauser: The Enigma of a Century*), he in fact eventually identified with the foundling to the point of formulating a paranoid ideation modelled on Hauser's demise, one of being pursued by a knife-bearing stranger. Like Christ, Helian, Elis and Sebastian—each a Trakl subject with a nebulous identity on the tightrope between Trakl himself and a mythical No One—Caspar Hauser intrigued Trakl because he represented the pre-fall innocence of man (an innocence Trakl symbolized with the color blue), and a perceptual rather than conceptual approach to reality. In his infinite innocence and naiveté Caspar Hauser was "not yet born"—not yet corrupted by the world of man—while Trakl, in his own words, was "only half born." Trakl makes the telling and definitive link between himself and Caspar Hauser when he states quite explicitly, in a letter to Buschbeck, "I shall always remain a poor Caspar Hauser." Trakl will always remain, that is, outside of the community of men, lost on earth, doomed to the haunt of a strange vision, and longing to return to the Caspar-state of innocense, the blue cave, which he forfeited in acts epitomized by his incest with Grete. Hauser and the other alter egos one finds in Trakl's poetry represent not only Trakl's longing to undo the evils of his past, but also, and simultaneously, the defeating realization that the ends of such longing are unattainable. While one Trakl propagates the return to Eden on earth, another Trakl—the stronger and less optimistic one—establishes in his poetry the precedents for early death which "preserves" the idealized " image of man." Christ, Helian, Elis, Sebastian and Caspar Hauser, in other words, provide not only subject matter for Trakl's poem-penance, but also rationale for the meaningful cessation of his tortured life. Each of these alter egos has "the quiet god close his blue eyelids over him"; each has his silence make sense. Trakl's poetry appropriates the innocence and "salvation" of the subjects peopling the otherwordly romance that attracted him increasingly as a means to glorify his undefeatable gloom.

The Trakl/Hauser affinity offers the greatest insight into the source of Trakl's poetry when we follow the lead of Peter Handke's 1968 drama *Kaspar* and suggest that language bears the ultimate responsibility for the loss of innocense. One is drawn out of the perceptual, unnamed One-world by language and then made to not only function in a cognitive mode that artificially orders a world with grammar, but also to there be manipulated by the very instrument (language itself) which one had intended to master rather than serve. The process of self-discovery initiated by the acquisition of the pronoun *I* results in the termination of the not-yet-born state which Trakl idealized in Caspar Hauser. Through language one eventually becomes one's self, it seems, an event in many cases unbearable enough without being complicated by the lingering aftermath of reflection that self-consciousness demands, without being doomed, as we must, to the fact that "One becomes one's self" implies two distinct beings, neither of which we fully or truly are.

Being "unborn" is indeed more comfortable. The fall into self-consciousness—downward and downward "to the stars," to borrow Trakl's inversion—is in many cases horrifying enough to make suicide seem the brightest alternative. If schizophrenia (Trakl's Cracow diagnosis read "dementia praecox," a classification which evolved into the current schizophrenias) indeed has its source in the earliest stages of childhood—in, specifically, a child's failure to adequately resolve his symbiotic relationship with his mother and to evolve a fully realized and independent *I*—then each individual suffering from this disorder must found his existence on a hollow *I* pursuing the mandates of an inexact point of view, and on the theses and formulations resulting from this view-point's unknowing commitment to an interesting piece of etymology: "I know," in Greek, is the present perfect of "I see." Faulty perception, thus, becomes conception in both of its signi-fications: meaning (or poetry) is born of error. In this scheme all of one's constructs, all of one's certitudes are products of invalid premises. Self-discovery in these cases—cases for which the Caspar legend serves as paradigm—is not an illuminating and rewarding enterprise, but rather a nightmare that shatters one's previous un-derstanding of reality and, with it, one's self. "The symbol of madness," Michel Foucault has summarized,

> will henceforth be that mirror which, without reflecting anything real, will secretly offer the man who observes himself in it the dream of his own presumption.

The dream, in this case, is the poetry. Trakl sees not the world but rather a narcissistic reconstruction of reality designed to facilitate his attempt to survive. The attempt fails because his aesthetic struggle to construct an Eden of his gloom is only feigned, is only a pretense to disguise his commitment to the reflection in Foucault's mirror; the poetry is designed only to postpone the inevitable and to encapsulate the gloom in a vacuum or limbo buffered with the resonance of sonics. "I bowed over the silent water [mirror]," Trakl wrote, and "I saw my face had abandoned me. And the white voice spoke to me: Kill yourself!" In a letter to Buschbeck Rilke suggested his recognition of Trakl's pronounced commit-ment to the Reflection by comparing Trakl to Li Po, a Chinese poet who drowned after drunkenly reaching from a boat for the moon (his face) reflecting from the water. Here is Trakl's fall downward "to the stars"; he had nothing to employ in an attempt to stay sane but the same language that initiated his pathetic decline into "the mirror of dead water."

A.F. Bance has pointed out that "Caspar's self-discovery is followed by annihilation of the personality," and that "The process of Caspar's growing self-awareness is inexorably accom-panied by sinister threats to his existence." Herzog pursues this theme in *Every Man for Himself*: Hauser is killed as he approaches self-awareness in order to prevent him from discovering his true identity. The life of Georg Trakl follows the Caspar Hauser master plot closely, but assumes both roles implied by "One becomes one's self" because Trakl internalizes the pursuer—often via paranoid ideation—and hunts himself. "The solution for someone like myself consists of going forward to one's self," he says, but the optimism of this solution finally declines into the premise "Always

18

the Self is black and near." Trakl makes the ominous knife-wielding stranger a part of himself, the part driving him into the depths of the Reflection, into the poetry that retreats—in this case much to its credit—from meaning to mythos and melos.

Standing before a mounted calf's head at a peasants' festival celebrating the consecration of a church, Georg Trakl, shivering and apparently dumbstruck, uttered "That is our Lord Christ." It is significant that the head was a calf's rather than a cow's, that the beast's early death was formalized by the mount, and that this trophy's status as a prize forced it to symbolize the consecration. More significant, however, is the fact that this utterance taken seriously indicates a degree of insanity sufficient to undermine the rationality of both the speaker and the interlocutor who would attempt to interpret it reasonably. Whatever "meaning" we attribute to "That is our Lord Christ," or to the Trakl canon it epitomizes, must result from an appreciation of the dynamics of language and lunacy far more than from the niceties of exegeses. "Confronted by a human being who impresses us as great," Lou Salomé once wrote concerning Freud, "should we not be moved rather than chilled by the knowledge that he might have attained his greatness only through his frailties." In Trakl's case we should be thoroughly grateful, for the poetry owes much to the pathology.

POEMS

Translated by
Robert Grenier,
Michael Hamburger,
David Luke
&
Christopher Middleton

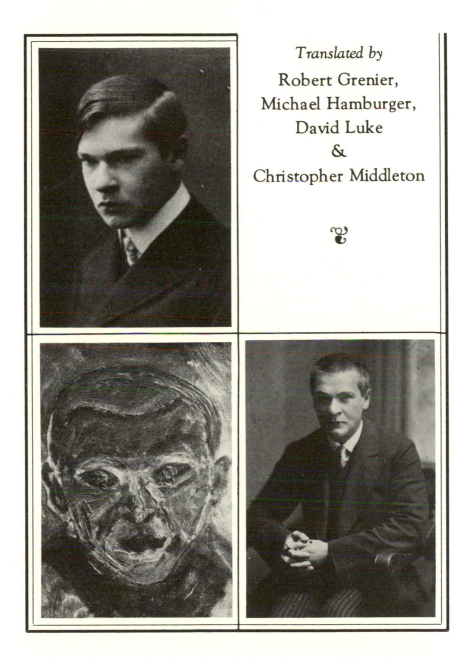

MUSIC IN THE MIRABEL

A fountain sings. White, gentle clouds, aglow,
Hang in pure azure. Slowly, pondering
And very silent, men and women go
Through the old garden in the evening.

The marble of our forebears has turned grey.
A flight of birds fades off beyond the park.
A faun with his dead eyes looks fixedly
At shadows that glide off into the dark.

From ancient trees the russet foliage falls
And through the open window, circling, drifts.
A flint lights up inside the room, appals
With many a phantom shape that twists and shifts.

A stranger comes into the house, all white.
Through mouldering passages a mastiff bounds.
Softly a maid puts out the last lamp's light.
At night the ear dwells on sonata sounds.

[M.H.]

DE PROFUNDIS

There is a stubble field on which a black rain falls.
There is a tree which, brown, stands lonely here.
There is a hissing wind which haunts deserted huts—
How sad this evening.

Past the village pond
The gentle orphan still gathers scanty ears of corn.
Golden and round her eyes are grazing in the dusk
And her lap awaits the heavenly bridegroom.

Returning home
Shepherds found the sweet body
Decayed in the bramble bush.

A shade I am remote from sombre hamlets.
The silence of God
I drank from the woodland well.

On my forehead cold metal forms.
Spiders look for my heart.
There is a light that fails in my mouth.

At night I found myself upon a heath,
Thick with garbage and the dust of stars.
In the hazel copse
Crystal angels have sounded once more.

[M.H.]

MANKIND

Round gorges deep with fire arrayed, mankind;
A roll of drums, dark brows of warriors marching;
Footsteps in fog of blood, black metals grind;
Despair, sad night of thought, despair high-arching;
Eve's shadow falls, halloo of hunt, red coin consigned.
Cloud, broken by light, the Supper's end;
This bread, this wine, have silence in their keeping.
Here do the Twelve assembled, numbered, stand;
They cry out under olive trees at night, half-sleeping.
Into the wound Saint Thomas dips his hand.

[C.M.]

TOWARDS NIGHTFALL MY HEART

At nightfall one hears the crying of bats,
Two black horses frisk in the meadow,
The red maple rustles.
To the wanderer the little wayside inn appears.
Glorious new wine and walnuts taste to him,
Glorious: to stagger drunk through the dusking wood.
In its black branches the grievous bells are pealing,
Dew-drops fall on his face.

[M.H.]

ROSARY SONGS

TO MY SISTER

Where you walk, there it is autumn and evening,
A blue deer under trees and its music,
A lonely pond in the evening.

The flight of birds and its soft music,
Sadness settling over your eyes' curve.
Your slight smile and its music.

God has altered your eyelids' curve.
O Good Friday's child, at night stars seek
Your forehead's curve.

[D.L.]

NEARNESS OF DEATH

O the evening deep in the sombre hamlets of childhood.
The pond beneath the willows
Fills with the tainted sighs of sadness.

O the wood which softly lowers its brown eyes,
When from the solitary's bony hands
The purple of his enraptured days ebbs down.

O the nearness of death. Let us pray.
This night the delicate limbs of lovers
Yellowed with incense on warm pillows untwine.

[M.H.]

AMEN

Corruption gliding through the crumbled room;
Shadows on yellow hangings; in dark mirrors
The ivory sorrow of our hands is arched.

Brown beads trickle through fingers that have died
In the stillness
An angel's blue opium eyes unclose.

The evening also is blue;
The hour of our decease, the shadow of Azrael
Darkening a little brown garden.

[D.L.]

TRUMPETS

Under trimmed willows, where tanned children play
And leaves blow, tone trumpets. A churchyard shudder.
Banners of scarlet crash through the maples' grief,
Riders along ryefields, empty mills.

Or shepherds sing at night and stags step
Into the circle of their fire, the grove's ancient sorrow,
Dancers fling themselves up from a black wall;
Banners of scarlet, laughter, insanity, trumpets.

[R.G.]

THE RATS

In the courtyard the autumn moon shines white.
From the roof's edge wild shadows drop.
A silence lives in empty windows,
Easily up into which leap the rats

And flit hissing here and there—
A greyish dust-haze reeks
After them from the latrine, through which
The spectral moonshine shivers.

And they scramble greedily, insanely
And overflow house and sheds
Full of grain, fruit.
In the dark icy winds whine.

[R.G.]

HELIAN

I

In the lonely hours of the spirit,
Beautiful it is to walk in the sun,
Beside the yellow walls of the summer.
Softly the footfalls ring in the grass; but always
The son of Pan sleeps in the grey marble.

Evenings on the terrace we got drunk with brown wine.
Reddish the peach glows in the leaves;
Gentle sonata, happy laughing.

Beautiful is the quiet of the night.
On a dark plain
We meet with shepherds and white stars.

When autumn has come
Sober clearness enters the grove.
Calmed we wander beside red walls
And the round eyes follow the flight of birds.
At nightfall the white water sinks in funeral jars.

In bare branches heaven celebrates.
In pure hands the countryman carries bread and wine
And the fruits ripen peacefully in the sunny larder.

O how earnest is the countenance of the dear dead.
Yet a just regard delights the soul.

II

Immense is the silence of the ravaged garden
When the young novice garlands his temples with brown leaves,
His breath drinks icy gold.

The hands stir the age of bluish waters
Or in cold night the white cheeks of the sisters.

Soft and harmonious is a walk past friendly rooms,
Where solitude is, and the rustling of the maple tree,
Where still perhaps the thrush is singing.

Beautiful is man and evident in the darkness,
When marvelling he moves his arms and legs
And silent in purple caves the eyes roll.

At vespers the stranger is lost in black November destruction,
Under rotted boughs, beside leprous walls
Where earlier the holy brother walked,
Sunk in the faint thrumming of his madness.

O how lonely the evening wind desists.
Fading, the head bows in the dark of the olive tree.

III

Overwhelming is the generation's decline,
At this hour the eyes of him who gazes
Fill with the gold of his stars.

At nightfall bells die that will chime no more,
The black walls on the square decay,
To prayer the dead soldier calls.

A pale angel
The son steps into the empty house of his fathers.

The sisters have gone far away to white old men,
At night the sleeper found them under the columns in the hall,
Returned from their sorrowful pilgrimages.

O how their hair curds with filth and worms
When he plants his silver feet therein,
And from bare rooms they move with dead steps.

O you psalms in fiery midnight rains,
When the servants with nettles thrashed the gentle eyes,
The childlike fruits of the elder tree
Marvelling stoop over an empty grave.

Softly yellowed moons roll
Over the fever sheets of the young man,
Before silence of winter comes.

IV

A high destiny ponders down Kidron passing,
Where the cedar, tender being,
Unfolds beneath the blue brows of the father,
Over the meadow at night a shepherd leads his flock.
Or there are cries in sleep
When in the grove a brazen angel advances on man
And the saint's flesh melts on the glowing grill.

Round the clay huts purple vines abound,
Sonorous sheaves of yellowed corn,
The hum of bees, the flight of the crane.
At nightfall the resurrected meet on mountain paths.

Lepers are mirrored in black waters
Or they part their filth-bespattered robes,
Weeping to the wind that blows with balm from the rosy hill.

Slim girls grope through the alleys of night,
To find the loving shepherd.
On Saturdays quiet singing sounds in the huts.

Let the song also remember the boy,
His madness, and white temples and his departing,
The mouldered boy, who opens bluish his eyes.
O how sorrowful is this meeting again.

V

The stairs of madness in black rooms,
The shadows of the old men under the open door,
When Helian's soul regards itself in the rosy mirror
And snow and leprosy slide from his temples.

On the walls the stars have been extinguished
And the white forms of the light.

From the tapestry bones of the graves descend,
The silence of decayed crosses on the hill,
Sweetness of incense in the purple night wind.

O you crushed eyes in black mouths,
When the grandson in his mind's gentle night,
Lonely, ponders the darker ending,
The quiet god closes his blue eyelids over him.

[C.M.]

TO THE BOY ELIS

Elis, when the ouzel calls in the black wood,
This is your own decline.
Your lips drink in the coolness of the blue
Spring in the rocks.

No more, when softly your forehead bleeds,
Primaeval legends
And dark interpretation of the flight of birds.

But you walk with soft footsteps into the night
Which is laden with purple grapes,
And move your arms more beautifully in the blue.

A thorn-bush sounds
Where your lunar eyes are.
O Elis, how long you have been dead.

Your body is a hyacinth
Into which a monk dips his waxen fingers.
Our silence is a black cavern

From which at times a gentle animal
Steps out and slowly lowers heavy lids.
Upon your temples black dew drips,

The last gold of perished stars.

[M.H.]

ELIS

I

Absolute is the stillness of this golden day.
Under old oak trees,
Elis, you appear, one resting with round eyes.

Their blueness reflects the sleeping of lovers.
Against your mouth
Their rosy sighs died down.

At nightfall the fisherman hauled in his heavy nets.
A good shepherd
Leads his flock along the forest edge.
Oh how righteous, Elis, are all your days.

Softly sinks
The olive tree's blue stillness on bare walls,
An old man's dark song subsides.

A golden boat
Sways, Elis, your heart against a lonely sky.

II

A gentle chiming of bells resounds in Elis' breast
At nightfall,
When to the black pillow his head sinks down.

A blue deer
Bleeds in the thorny thicket quietly.

Aloof and separate a brown tree stands,
Its blue fruits have fallen away.

Symbols and stars
Softly go down in the evening pond.

Behind the hill winter has come.

At night
Blue doves drink the icy sweat
That trickles from Elis' crystal brow.

Always
God's lonely wind sounds on black walls.

[M.H.]

CHILDHOOD

Full-berried the elder-bush; tranquilly childhood lived
In a blue cave. Over the bygone path
Where now pale brown the wild grasses hiss,
Calm branches ponder; the rustling of leaves

This too when blue waters sound under the crags.
Gentle the blackbird's plaint. A shepherd
Follows unspeaking the sun that rolls from the autumn hill.

A blue moment is purely and simply soul.
At the forest edge a shy deer shows itself, at peace
Below in the vale the old bells and sombre hamlets rest.

Now more devout, you know the meaning of the dark years,
Coolness and autumn in solitary rooms;
And still in holy azure shining footfalls ring.

An open window softly knocks; tears come
At the sight of the decayed graveyard on the hill,
Memory of told legends; yet the soul sometimes brightens
When she thinks of the glad folk, the dark-gold springtime days.

[C.M.]

WAYFARING

At nightfall they carried the stranger dead into the house;
An odour of tar; the red plane trees' soft rustling;
The dark flutter of jackdaws; the guard paraded on the square.
The sun has sunk in black linen; time and again this bygone
 evening returns.

In the next room my sister is playing a Schubert sonata.
Very softly her smile sinks into the decayed fountain,
Which rustles blue in the twilight. O how old our family is.
Someone whispers down in the garden; someone has left this black
 heaven.
The scent of apples up on the cupboard. Grandmother is lighting
 golden candles.

O how mild the autumn is. Soft our footsteps in the old park
Sound under lofty trees. O how earnest is the hyacinthine face of
 twilight.
The blue spring at your feet, mysterious your mouth's red stillness,
Enshadowed by slumber of leaves, by the dark gold of decayed
 sunflowers.

Your eyelids are heavy with poppy and dream softly against my
 forehead.
Gentle bells tremble through the heart. A blue cloud,
Your face has sunk over me in the twilight.

A song for the guitar, sounding in a strange tavern,
Wild elder-bushes there, a long bygone day in November,
Familiar steps on the dusky stair, the sight of beams tanned
 brown,
An open window, at which a sweet hope stayed behind—
Unspeakable it all is, O God, one is overwhelmed and falls on
 one's knees.

O how dark this night is. A purple flame
Failed at my mouth. In the stillness
The alarmed soul's lonely music fades and dies.
No more, when the wine-drunk head sinks down to the gutter.

[C.M.]

SEBASTIAN IN DREAM

Mother bore this infant in the white moon,
In the nut tree's shade, in the ancient elder's,
Drunk with the poppy's juice, the thrush's lament;
And mute
With compassion a bearded face bowed down to that woman,

Quiet in the window's darkness; and ancestral heirlooms,
Old household goods,
Lay rotting there; love and autumnal reverie.

So dark was the day of the year, desolate childhood,
When softly the boy to cool waters, to silver fishes walked down,
Calm and countenance;
When stony he cast himself down where black horses raced,
In the grey of the night his star possessed him.

Or holding his mother's icy hand
He walked at nightfall across St Peter's autumnal churchyard,
While a delicate corpse lay still in the bedroom's gloom
And he raised cold eyelids towards it.

But he was a little bird in leafless boughs,
The churchbell rang in dusking November,
His father's stillness, when asleep he descended the dark of the
          turning stair.

Peace of the soul. A lonely winter evening.
The dark shapes of shepherds by the ancient pond;
Little child in the hut of straw; O how softly
Into black fever his face sank down.
Holy night.

Or holding his father's horny hand
In silence he walked up Calvary Hill
And in dusky rock recesses
The blue shape of Man would pass through His legend,
Blood ran purple from the wound beneath His heart.
O how softly the Cross rose up in the dark of his soul.

Love; when in black corners the snow was melting,
Gaily a little blue breeze was caught in the ancient elder,
In the nut tree's vault of shade;
And in silence a rosy angel appeared to that boy;

Gladness; when in cool rooms a sonata sounded at nightfall,
Among dark-brown beams
A blue butterfly crept from its silver chrysalis.

O the nearness of death. From the stony wall
A yellow head bowed down, silent that child,
Since in that month the moon decayed.

Rose-coloured Easter bell in the burial vault of the night,
And the silver voices of stars,
So that madness, dark and shuddering, ebbed from the sleeper's
                brow.

O how quiet to ramble along the blue river's bank,
To ponder forgotten things when in leafy boughs
The thrush's call brought strangeness into a world's decline.

Or holding an old man's bony hand
In the evening he walked to the crumbling city walls,
And in his black greatcoat carried a rosy child,
In the nut tree's shade the spirit of evil appeared.

Groping his way over the green steps of summer. O how softly
In autumn's brown stillness the garden decayed,
Scent and sadness of the ancient elder,
When the silver voice of the angel died down in Sebastian's
       shadow.

[M.H.]

NOCTURNE

Breath of the One Unmoved. Animal face
Frozen with azure, with its sanctity.
Immense the power of silence in stone.

The mask of a night bird. A quiet triad
Fades on one sound. Elai! your countenance
Inclines unspeaking over the pale-blue waters.

O you calm mirrors of the truth.
On the ivory cheeks of the lonely one appears
Reflected the splendour of fallen angels.

[C.M.]

ON THE MOORS

Wanderer in black wind; lightly the dry reed
Whispers in the stillness of the moor. Under grey heavens
A flight of wild birds passes,
Crosswise, over dark water.

Uproar. In ruined cottages
On black wings, foulness flaps up;
Crippled birches creak in the wind.

Evening in the abandoned tavern. The gentle melancholy
Of grazing herds encloses the way home,
Apparition of Night: toads plunge out of silvery waters.

[R.G.]

ON THE MÖNCHSBERG

Where the crumbling pathway descends in the shadow of autumn
    elms,
Far from the leafy huts, the sleeping shepherds,
The dark shape that came from the coolness still follows the
    wanderer

Over the footbridge of bone, and the boy's hyacinth voice
Softly reciting the forest's forgotten legend,
And more gently, a sick thing now, the brother's wild lament.

Thus a little green touches the knee of the stranger,
And his head that turned to stone;
Nearer, the blue spring murmurs the women's lamentation.

[D.L.]

CASPAR HAUSER SONG

For Bessie Loos

He truly adored the sun, as, crimson, it sank from the hill-top,
The paths of the forest, the blackbird singing
And the joy of green.

Serious was his habitation in the tree-shade
And pure his face.
God spoke a gentle flame into his heart:
O man!

His silent footstep found the city at evening;
The dark lament of his mouth:
I want to be a horseman.

But bush and beast pursued him,
House and twilit garden of pallid men
And his murderer sought him.

Beautiful the spring and summer and the autumn
Of the righteous man, his soft footfall
Beside the dark rooms of dreamers.
By night he stayed alone with his star;

Saw snow falling through bare branches
And in the dusking hall his murderer's shadow.

Silver it fell, the head of the not-yet-born.

[D.L.]

IN TRANSIT

Grain and grape have been cut,
The hamlet in autumn and peace.
Hammer and anvil clang incessantly,
Laughter in purple leaves.

Asters past dark hedges
Summon the pale child.
Say how long it is we have been dead;
The sun desires to shine black.

Little red fish in the fishpond;
Forehead, afraid, overhearing itself;
Evening wind against the window delicately rustles,
Blue organ grinding.

Secret sparkle of stars
Lets one look up once more.
Apparition of the mother in pain and horror;
Black mignonettes in the dark.

[R.G.]

THE FALL OF THE LONELY ONE

Again dark fall returns, replete with fruit, profusion,
The yellowed sheen of lovely summer days.
A clear blue steps from rotting husks;
The flight of birds whirrs with ancient myths.
Now wine's pressed, the mild stillness
Is filled with low-voiced answers to dark questions.

And here and there a cross upon a wasted hill; a herd
Disperses into red woods. Over the fishpond's
Mirror surface strays a cloud;
The farmer's quiet gesture is at rest.
So gently the blue flight of evening stirs,
A roof of dry straw, black earth.

Soon stars nestle in the tired one's eyebrows;
A quiet modesty in cool rooms faces about
And angels stalk noiselessly out of the blue
Eyes of lovers, who more gently suffer.
A rustling of reeds; a bony horror attacks
As black dew drips from bare willow boughs.

[R.G.]

REST AND SILENCE

Shepherds have buried the sun in the bare forest.
A fisherman has hauled
The moon in a fine-spun net from the freezing pond.

In a blue crystal,
Pallid, man dwells, and his cheek leans on his stars;
Or he bows his head in purple sleep.

Yet still by birds' black flight the visionary
Is touched, and by blue flowers' holiness,
And the near-by silence ponders forgotten things, extinguished
        angels.

Night envelops the brow once more amid lunar stones;
And a radiant youth
The sister appears amid autumn and black corruption.

[D.L.]

BIRTH

Mountains: blackness, silence and snow,
Red from the forest the hunt comes down;
O the mossy gaze of the wild deer.

The mother's stillness; under black pine trees
The sleeping hands extending open
When the cold moon appears in its decay.

O the birth of man. Nocturnal murmur
Blue waters rushing over the rock-bed;
Sighing the fallen angel espies his image,

Something pale wakes in a musty room.
Two moons,
The old stone woman's eyes are shining.

Ah how the mother cries in labour. With black wing
Night brushes the boy's cheek,
Snow that softly from purple cloud descends.

[C.M.]

DECLINE

To Karl Borromäus Heinrich

Over the white pond
The wild birds have travelled on.
In the evening an icy wind blows from our stars.

Over our graves
The broken brow of the night inclines.
Under oak trees we sway in a silver boat.

Always the town's white walls resound.
Under arches of thorns,
O my brother, blind minute-hands,
We climb towards midnight.

[M.H.]

TO ONE WHO DIED YOUNG

O the black angel who softly stepped from the heart of the tree
When we were gentle playmates in the evening,
By the edge of the pale-blue fountain.
Our step was easy, the round eyes in autumn's brown coolness,
O the purple sweetness of the stars.

But the other descended the stone steps of the Mönchsberg,
A blue smile on his face, and strangely ensheathed
In his quieter childhood, and died;
And the silver face of his friend stayed behind in the garden,
Listening in the leaves or in the ancient stones.

Soul sang of death, the green decay of the flesh,
And it was the murmur of the forest,
The fervid lament of the animals.
Always from dusky towers rang the blue evening bells.

Times came when the other saw shadows in the purple sun,
The shadows of putrescence in the bare branches;
At evening, when by the dusky wall the blackbird sang,
His ghost quietly appeared there in the room.

O the blood that runs from the throat of the musical one,
Blue flower; O the fiery tear
Wept into the night.

Golden cloud and time. In a lonely room
You ask the dead child to visit you more often,
You walk and talk together under elms by the green riverside.

[C.M.]

WESTERN SONG

O the soul's nocturnal wingbeat:
Shepherds we walked by dusky forests once
And the red deer followed, the green flower and babbling stream,
Humbly. O the ancient sound of the little cricket,
Blood flowering on the sacrificial slab
And the lonely birdcry over the pond's green calm.

O you crusades and glowing tortures
Of the flesh, descent of the crimson fruits
In the garden at evening where long ago the pious disciples
                 walked,
People now of war, from wounds and star-dreams waking.
O the gentle cornflower sheaf of night.

O you times of quietness and golden autumns
When peaceful monks we trod the purple grape;
And hill and forest shone around us.
O you hunts and castles; peace at evening,
When in his room man meditated justice,
Wrestled in dumb prayer for the living head of God.

O the bitter hour of decline,
When we regard a stony face in black waters.
But radiant the lovers raise their silver eyelids:
One kin. From rosy pillows incense pours
And the sweet canticle of the bodies resurrected.

[C.M.]

SOUTH WIND

Blind lamentation in the wind, moon-days of winter,
Childhood, softly footsteps fade by the dark hedge,
The long peal of bells in the evening.
Softly the pallid night approaches,

Transforms into purple dreams the pain and affliction
Of stony life,
That without abatement the thorn may goad the decaying body.

From the depths of its sleep the fear-stricken soul moans suddenly,

And the wind in the depths of broken trees,
And swaying, a shape of lamentation,
The mother moves through the lonely wood

Of this speechless grief; nights
Full of tears, nights full of fiery angels.
Silver, against a bare wall, a child's skeleton smashes.

[D.L.]

TO THE SILENCED

Oh, the great city's madness when at nightfall
The crippled trees gape by the blackened wall,
The spirit of evil peers from a silver mask;
Lights with magnetic scourge drive off the stony night.
Oh, the sunken pealing of evening bells.

Whore who in her icy spasms gives birth to a dead child.
With raving whips God's fury punishes brows possessed.
Purple pestilence, hunger that breaks green eyes.
Oh, the horrible laughter of gold.

But silent in dark caves a stiller humanity bleeds,
Out of hard metals moulds the redeeming head.

[M.H.]

LIMBO

By autumnal walls, shadows are searching there
For singing gold on the hill
Evening clouds that browse
In the withered plane trees' calm.
Darker tears this age exhales,
Perdition, when the dreamer's heart
Is overflowing with purple sunset,
With the dejection of the smoking town;
Golden cool blows from behind the traveller,
The stranger, from the graveyard,
As if a delicate corpse were shadowing him.

The stone building softly chimes;
The orphans' garden, the dark hospital,
A red ship on the canal.
Decaying men
Dreaming rise and fall in the dark
And from blackish doorways
Angels advance with cold foreheads;
Azure, the keening of mothers.
There rolls through her long hair
A fiery wheel, the round day,
Unending torture of the earth.

In cool rooms, without meaning,
Furniture rots, with bony hands
Unholy childhood
Fumbles in the blue for fairytales,
The plump rat gnaws cupboard and door,
A heart
Stiffens in snowy silence.
Echoes resound in decaying darkness,

The purple curses of hunger echoing,
The dark sword-blades of lies,
As if somewhere a brazen gate had slammed.

[C.M.]

THE SUN

Daily the yellow sun comes over the hill.
Lovely the forest is, the dark beast,
And man: huntsman or shepherd.

Ruddy the fish rises in the green pond.
Under the rounded heaven
The fisherman softly moves in a blue boat.

Grape ripens slowly, and the corn.
As day in stillness ends,
A good work and an evil is prepared.

When night comes,
The wanderer softly lifts his heavy eyelids.
Sun breaks from a sombre abyss.

[C.M.]

SUMMER

At evening, the sound of the cuckoo
Stops in the wood.
The grain bends lower,
The red poppy.

Black thunderclouds bloom
Above the hill.
The ancient song of the cricket
Fades off into the fields.

The leaves of the chestnut
Tree stir no more.
Upon the spiral staircase
Your dress rustles.

One silent candle shines
In the dark room;
A silvery hand
Extinguishes it;

No wind, no stars. Night.

[R.G.]

OCCIDENT

For Else Lasker-Schüler

I

Moon, as if a dead thing
Stepped out of a blue cave,
And many blossoms fall
Across the rocky path.
Silver a sick thing weeps
By the evening pond,
In a black boat
Lovers crossed over to death.

Or the footsteps of Elis
Ring through the grove
The hyacinthine
To fade again under oaks.
O the shape of that boy
Formed out of crystal tears,
Nocturnal shadows.
Jagged lightning illumines his temples
The ever-cool,
When on the verdant hill
Springtime thunder resounds.

II

So quiet are the green woods
Of our homeland,
The crystal wave
That dies against a perished wall
And we have wept in our sleep;

Wander with hesitant steps
Along the thorny hedge
Singers in the evening summer
In holy peace
Of the vineyards distantly gleaming;
Shadows now in the cool lap
Of night, eagles that mourn.
So quietly does a moonbeam close
The purple wounds of sadness.

III

You mighty cities
stone on stone raised up
in the plain!
So quietly
with darkened forehead
the outcast follows the wind,
bare trees on the hillside.
You rivers distantly fading!
Gruesome sunset red
is breeding fear
in the thunderclouds.
You dying peoples!
Pallid billow
that breaks on the beaches of Night,
stars that are falling.

[M.H.]

THE SOUL'S SPRINGTIME

A sudden cry in sleep; wind rushes through dark streets,
Azure of spring beckons through breaking branches,
Night's dew is purple, stars all round the sky are fading.
The river gleams green in the dusk, and silver the old avenues
And the spires of the city. O gentle drunkenness
In the gliding boat, O the dark calls of blackbirds
In childlike gardens. The rose-red veil disperses.

Solemnly the waters murmur. O the moist shadows on the
   meadow,
The animals walking; green things, a spray of blossoms
Touching the crystal brow; shimmering rocking boat.
Softly the sun sings through the rose-red clouds on the hill.
Great is the stillness of the pinewood, grave the shadows by the
   river.

Purity! Purity! Where are the terrible pathways of death,
Of grey stony silence, the rocks of the night
And the unquiet shades? A radiant pit of sunlight.
O my sister, when I found you by the lonely clearing
In the wood, at noon, in a great silence of all animals,
You were white under the wild oak, and the silver thorn-bush
   blossomed.
A mighty dying, and the singing flame in the heart.

Darker the waters flow round the fishes gracefully playing.
O hour of grief, O speechless gaze of the sun.
The soul is an alien thing upon earth. A dim religious
Azure descends on the mishewn forest, and a bell
Tolls from the village dark and long; they lead him to rest.
Silent the myrtle blooms over his dead white eyelids.

Softly the waters murmur in the declining afternoon.
On the river bank the green wilderness darkens, the rose-red wind
        rejoices;
A brother's gentle song on the evening hill.

[D.L.]

WINTER NIGHT

Snow has been falling. After midnight, drunk with purple wine,
you leave the dark district of men, the red flame of their hearth-
fires. O darkness!

Black frost. The earth is hard, the air tastes of bitterness. Your
stars conjoin to evil signs.

With petrified steps you stamp along the railway-track, with
rounded eyes, like a soldier storming a black redoubt. Avanti!

Bitter snow and moon!

A red wolf strangled by an angel. Your walking legs clash like
blue ice and a smile full of sadness and pride has petrified your
face and your brow grows pale with the voluptuous frost;

or silently stoops over the sleep of a watchman who lay down in
his wooden hut.

Frost and smoke. A white shirt of stars burns the shoulders that
wear it, and God's vultures tear the flesh of your metal heart.

O the stone hill. Silent and forgotten, the cool body melts away
in the silver snow.

The blackness of sleep. Far through the ice the ear follows the
paths of the stars.

When you woke, the bells in the village were ringing. The rose-
red silver day stepped through the eastern gate.

[D.L.]

IN HELLBRUNN

Following once again the evening's blue lament
Along the hillside, along the vernal pond—
As if the shades of those long dead, the shades
Of prelates and of noble women hovered over them—
Their flowers are blooming already, the earnest violets
In the evening's depth, the blue wellspring's
Crystal wave purls on. So religiously
Do the oaks grow green over forgotten paths of the dead,
The golden cloud over the pond.

[M.H.]

THE HEART

The wild heart turned white in the wood;
O the dark fear
Of death, when the gold
Died in a grey cloud.
November evening.
By the bare gate of the slaughterhouse there stood
The crowd of poor women.
Into every basket
Rank flesh and entrails fell;
Accursed fare!

The blue dove of nightfall
Brought no atonement.
Dark trumpet call
Rang through the elm trees'
Damp golden leaves,
A tattered banner
Steaming with blood,
So that wild in his sadness
A man gives heed.
O brazen ages
Buried there in the sunset red.

From the house's dark hall there stepped
The golden shape
Of the maiden-youth
Surrounded with pale moons
Of autumnal courtliness,
Black pine trees snapped
In the night gale,
The steep-walled fortress.
O heart
Glistening away into snowy coolness.

[M.H.]

SLEEP

Accursed you dark poisons,
White sleep!
This, the rarest of gardens
Of trees wrapped in twilight,
Filled with serpents, nocturnal moths,
Spiders and bats.
Stranger, your lost shadow
In the sunset's red,
A gloomy corsair
On the salt sea of sadness.
White birds on the hem of the night fly off
Over collapsing cities
Of steel.

[M.H.]

EVENING

With dead figures of heroes
The moon is filling
The silent forests
O sickle-moon!
And the mouldering rocks all round
With the soft embraces
Of lovers,
The phantoms of famous ages;
This blue light shines
Towards the city
Where a decaying race
Lives coldly and evilly,
Preparing the dark future
Of their white descendants.
O moon-wrapped shadows
Sighing in the empty crystal
Of the mountain lake.

[D.L.]

NIGHT

You, wild fissure, I sing
In the night's storm
Upon towering mountains;
You—grey tower dungeons
Overflowing with hellish grimaces,
Fiery animals, rough
Ferns, spruce,
Crystal flowers.
Interminable pain
So that you hunt God
Gentle spirit,
Deeply sighing in the waterfall,
In swaying Scotch fir.

Golden, the fire flares up
About the nations.
Over blackish cliffs, dead
Drunk, crashes
The luminous tornado,
The blue comber of
The glacier
And powerfully
Tolls the bell in the valley:
Flames, curses
And the dark
Play of lust—
A petrified head
Storms heaven.

[R.G.]

DEJECTION

Mighty you are, dark mouth
Within, configuration formed
Of autumn clouds,
Of golden evening stillness;
A greenishly glimmering mountain brook
In the shadow precinct
Of broken pines:
A village
That in brown images piously suffers decay.

There the black horses leap
On a hazy pasture.
You soldiers!
From the hill where dying the sun rolls
Laughing blood roars down—
Under oaks,
Speechless. O the army's
Grim dejection; a bright helmet
Clattering slid from a crimson brow.

Autumn night so coolly comes.
Lights up with stars
Above the broken bones of men
The quiet maiden monk.

[M.H.]

HOMECOMING

The dark years' coolness,
Pain and hope
Confirmed by Cyclopean stone,
Abandoned mountains, gold
Breath of fall,
Evening clouds—
Clarity!

Crystalline childhood gazes
From blue eyes;
Below dark spruce—
Love, hope;
So that, out of fiery eyelids,
Dew drips into stiff grass
Uncheckably!

Look! the golden footbridge
Shattering into the snow
Of the abyss!
The night valley
Breathes blue coolness—
Faith, hope!
Lonely churchyard, greetings.

[R.G.]

EASTERN FRONT

The wrath of the people is dark,
Like the wild organ notes of winter storm,
The battle's crimson wave, a naked
Forest of stars.

With ravaged brows, with silver arms
To dying soldiers night comes beckoning.
In the shade of the autumn ash
Ghosts of the fallen are sighing.

Thorny wilderness girdles the town about.
From bloody doorsteps the moon
Chases terrified women.
Wild wolves have poured through the gates.

[C.M.]

LAMENT

Sleep and death, the dark eagles
Around this head swoop all night long:
Eternity's icy wave
Would swallow the golden image
Of man; against horrible reefs
His purple body is shattered.
And the dark voice laments
Over the sea.
Sister of stormy sadness,
Look, a timorous boat goes down
Under stars,
The silent face of the night.

[M.H.]

GRODEK

At nightfall the autumn woods cry out
With deadly weapons and the golden plains,
The deep blue lakes, above which more darkly
Rolls the sun; the night embraces
Dying warriors, the wild lament
Of their broken mouths.
But quietly there in the willow dell
Red clouds in which an angry god resides,
The shed blood gathers, lunar coolness.
All the roads lead to blackest carrion.
Under golden twigs of the night and stars
The sister's shade now sways through the silent copse
To greet the ghosts of the heroes, the bleeding heads;
And softly the dark flutes of autumn sound in the reeds.
O prouder grief! You brazen altars,
Today a great pain feeds the hot flame of the spirit,
The grandsons yet unborn.

[M.H.]

PROSE POEMS

Translated by
Roderick Iverson

TRANSFORMATION OF EVIL

Autumn: black footfall at the forest's edge; a moment of mute disruption; beneath barren trees a leper's forehead is eavesdropping. An evening of the distant past now settles over the mossy steps; November. A bell tolls and a cluster of red and black horses are guided into the village by their groom. Beneath a hazel thicket the huntsman, green, rips the guts out of some untamed creature, his hands smoking from blood, and the shadow of the animal sighs in the foliage above his eyes, brown and silently; the wood. Crows disperse across the air, three of them, their flight like a sonata, full of faded chords and manly sorrow; a golden cloud gently dissolves. By the mill boys kindle a fire. Flame is brother to the palest among them, he laughs buried in purple hair; or it's a precinct of murder past which a stony path leads. The yellow-blossoming berry trees have vanished now—a perennial dream in the leaden wind beneath pines; fear, green darkness, the gurgling sounds of someone being drowned: from the starry pond the fisherman pulls an immense black fish, face full of madness, cruelty. The speaking sonority of reeds, bickering men in the background are swayed in a red boat over the icy autumn water by one who lives in the dark legend of his time, one whose eyes have loomed open, crystalline, above the nights, above the virginal terror. Evil.

What is it compels you to linger on the ruined stair, in the house of your fathers? Leaden blackness. What is it that you raise to your eyes with a silvery hand, and your lids sinking down as though drunk from the poppy? But through the wall of stone you see the starry heavens, the Milky Way, Saturn; red. In a raging delirium, the barren tree raps against the wall of stone. You on the ruined steps: tree, star, stone! You, a blue creature that gently shivers—you, the pale priest who at a black altar puts the ritual knife to its neck. O your smile in the darkness, sad and evil, that makes a child blanch in sleep. A red flame sprang from your hand charring the winged insects of the night. O flute of light, flute of death. What was it that still compelled you to linger on the ruined stair in the house of your fathers? Below, at the gate, an angel knocks with a crystal finger.

O the hells of sleep, dark alleyways, a tiny brown garden. The dead figurine intones softly in the blue evening. Little green flowers flutter around the shape of her whose face is gone; or it bends down faded over a murderer's cold forehead in the darkness of a hallway. Prayer and adoration, the purple flames of lust—a sleeper's dying plunge over black stairs into darkness.

Someone abandoned you at the crossroads and for a long time your gaze travels backwards; a silver step in the shadow of deformed apple trees. Purple gleams the fruit on black branches and in the grass the snake sloughs off its skin. O, the darkness, the sweat that forms on an icy brow, and the saddened dreams in wine beneath smoke-blackened beams in the village tavern. You, still a wilderness, conjure rosy islands from out of the brown mists of tobacco smoke, and, from inward marrow, you clench a griffin's wild shriek as he hunts in sea, storm and ice around the black cliffs. You, a green metal, and within, a fiery face that wants out, that wants to sing of dark seasons from the carrioned gallows mound, and the flaming fall of an angel. O, the despair that cracks to its knee with a mute scream!

One of the dead visits you. Blood from a suicide flows from that heart and in the blackness of his brow nests an unspeakable instant—this dark encounter. You—a purple moon when that other one appears in the green shadows of an olive tree. Followed by intransient night.

DREAM AND DERANGEMENT

In the evening father became an old man; in dark rooms mother's
face turned to stone and the curse of the blighted race fell burden-
some on the boy. Sometimes he'd remember his childhood, full of
sickness, dread and sullen darkness, muffled play in the star garden, or that he'd been feeding rats in that courtyard of partial
light. From a blue mirror stepped the gaunt presence of his sister
and he plunged as though dead into the darkness. At night his
mouth would break open like a red fruit and stars glimmered over
his mute distress. His dreams filled the old house of his ancestry
and evenings he enjoyed walking through graveyards crumbled
into ruin, or he'd gaze at the corpse in that room reserved for the
dead, the ripening flecks of decay on those beautiful hands. In the
doorway of a monastery he begged for bread; the shadow of a
stallion sprang from the darkness shaking him with terror. With
autumn, a seer of visions, he'd pass into the brown marshlands. O
the tranced hours of rapture, evenings along the river awakening
green, the chase. O soul that gently sang the song of reeds become
yellow; fiery piety. Serenity and calmness and his gaze but deep
into the star-eyes of that toad, and he felt the coolness of old stone
with his trembling hands and breathed life to the venerate speaking of blue streams. O the silver fish and the fruit that drops from
distorted trees. The chordal measure of his footsteps filled him
with pride and with a disdain for things human. Coming home, he
came across an uninhabited castle. Withered gods stood in the garden, grieving into evening. But to him it seemed: I was living here
forgotten years. The hymnal trill of an organ filled him with fear
and trembling—God's. And he passed his days in a dark pit, lied
and stole and hid himself—a flaming wolf—from the white face of
his mother. O the hours when with stony mouth he'd sink down
into the starry garden—and the shadow of a murderer overcame
him. With brow blazoned crimson he went down into the moor
and God's fury punished his metal shoulders—O birch trees in
storms, the phantom creatures of darkness that avoided his
maddened course. Hate seared his heart, and lust, when in the
flourishing summer garden he raped the quiet child, and, reflected
in the afterglow, saw that profound darkness, his own face. O the
sadness—an evening by the window when death, a gruesome
skeleton, stepped from purple flowers. O you towers and bells, and

night's shadows fell on him like stones.

No one loved him. In rooms merged of dissolving light his fiery head consummated deceit and lechery. The blue rustling of a woman's dress left him trembling numb, a frozen pillar, and in the doorway stood his mother's dark complexity. And the shadows of evil rose up about his head. O you nights and stars! Evenings he'd go up the mountain with the cripple; the sunset's rosy sheen lay over the icy summit and his heart toned gently in the diminished light. Stormy fir trees sank heavily over them and a red hunter appeared from the wood. When night fell his heart shattered crystalline and darkness pounded at his brow. Beneath barren oaks he strangled a wild cat in his icy hands. To the right, reverberant in sadness, there appeared the white form of an angel, and the shadow of the cripple loomed larger in the darkness. But he picked up a stone and threw it in that direction and there was a howling as the thing fled, and in the shadow of a tree the gentle face of the angel dissolved with a sigh. For hours he lay on the rocky ground gazing up in astonishment at the golden tent of stars. Chased by bats, he plunged headlong into the darkness. Breathless, he entered the ruined house. In the courtyard, he—a savage beast—drank from the fountain's blue waters until he froze. In a fever, he sat on the icy steps raging against God and begging for death. O the grey face of terror when he lifted those rounded eyes over the dove's slit throat. Scuttling across strange steps he met a heavily rouged Jewess and he grabbed at her black hair and seized her by the mouth. Fiends followed him through the gloomy alleyways and an iron clattering ripped apart his ear. An altarboy, he quietly followed the silent priest along autumnal walls; beneath lifeless trees he drunkenly inhaled the scarlet of those venerable robes. O the ruined disc of the sun. Sweet torments ate away his flesh. In a deserted byway his own bloody complexity rose before him, towering stiffly from the rubbish. But more deeply did he love the sublime workings of stone, the tower that with hellish grimaces nightly storms the blue starry heavens, and the cool grave where the fiery heart of man is sustained. O sadness, the unspeakable guilt made evident. But when, intent on some blazing gleam, he descended that autumn stream beneath leafless trees, there rose before him a flaming demon cloaked in a mantel of hair, the sister. Wakening, they were extinguished, those stars at that head.

O blighted race, accursed genealogy. When, in stained rooms, each fate is accomplished, death enters the house with its mouldering stride. Would that it were springtime outside and that in the blossoming tree a pleased bird were warbling. But the sparse green withers horribly at the window of those raised on darkness and sanguinary hearts continue to brood on evil. O the dim springtime routes of one who spends himself in ponderous thought. More justly does the blossoming hedge please him, the countryman's fresh harvest and the singing bird, God's gentle creature; the bell at evening and the beloved common properties, the community of man. That he might forget his fate and that thorny sting. The brook becomes an unfettered green where his silvered foot turns, and a fabulous tree rustles above his enclouded mind. So it is that he lifts the snake in his slight hand—and his heart melted away in a fire of tears. Sublime is the silence of the wood, the darkness become green, and the mossy creatures that flutter upwards as night descends. O the horror as each one knows its guilt, traveling the thorny path. So, in bramble underbrush, he found the white form of the child bleeding after the cloak of her recent spouse. But he stood mute and pained before her, buried in his steely hair. O radiant angels dispersed by night's purple wind. And he dwelt the entirety of night in that crystal cave and leprosy dilated across his silvery brow. A shadow, he descended the mountain trail beneath autumn stars. Snow fell and a gloomy blueness filled the house. His father's hard voice rang out like something blind and spelled an incantation to terror. O sadness, the stooped apparition of the women. Beneath stiffened hands, fruit and the alarmed family's household things crumbled away. A wolf ripped apart the first-born and the sisters fled into dark gardens to bony old men. A seer cloaked in darkness, he sang along the ruined walls and God's wind swallowed his voice. O death and its tender lust. O you children, inheritors of a dark line. The evil flowers of that blood gleam silvery at his temple, that cold moon in his shattered eyes. O people of the night! O the accursed!

Deep is the slumber in dark poisons, filled with stars and the white face—the mother's—of stone. Bitter is death, the fare of those laden with guilt; in the brown outgrowths of the central root the earthen countenance, grinning, crumbled away. But, on wakening from evil dreams, he sang gently in the green shadows of elderberry trees; sweet companion of childhood—a rosy angel approached him, so that, a gentle creature, he dozed off into the night, and he saw the starry face of purity. With the coming of summer the sunflowers, golden, sank down over the garden fence.

O the diligence of bees and the nut tree's green foliage, storms that pass. And the silver blossoming of the poppy that carries night's star dreams in its green capsule. O how still the house when father moved off into darkness. Fruit ripened purple on the tree and the gardener flexed his harsh hands. O those hair-shirted symbols in the glaring sun. Yet, with evening, the shadow of a dead man stepped quietly into the grieving circle of his family and his step rang crystalline over the green meadow by the wood. People of silence, they gathered at the table; dying ones, they broke the bread with waxen hands—bread that bleeds. O the sadness, the stony eyes of the sister when, at the meal, her madness erupted from the brother's clouded brow, and beneath the mother's troubled hands the bread turned to stone. O people of corruption, that with silver tongues they remained silent in that hell. The lamps in that cold room died out and, from purple masks, they gazed on at one another in pain and in silence. All night long rain plummeted down nourishing the fields. In that thorny wilderness a dark one followed the yellow pathways through the grain, the song of the lark and the gentle stillness of green branches, that he might find peace. O you towns and mossy steps, blazing thought. But at the forest edge his steps stagger bonily over sleeping snakes and the ear continues to follow the vulture's raving shriek. In the evening he found a bleak solitude in the rocks—someone dead to escort him into his father's dark house. A purple cloud enveloped his head so that, in silence, he swooped down on his own blood and image, a moonly face; and he sank stonily down into vacancy, when, in a shattered mirror, there appeared a dying youth, the sister—and night devoured the accursed generation.

REVELATION AND DEMISE

Strange are the nighttime pathways of man. As a sleepwalker I passed into the stony rooms and in each there burned a small and tranquil lamp, a copper candlestick, and when, frozen, I sank down to the couch, the black shadows of a strange woman stood again at the regal head, and I silently concealed my face in the slow hands. Hyacinths, likewise, had blossomed blue from the window and from the purple lips of a boundless breathing rose the old prayer, descended from the lids of crystal tears cried over a bitter world. In this hour I was the white son of my father's death. From the hill, in shivering blue showers, came the night wind, dark lamentation of the mother fading once again, and I saw black hell in my heart; a moment of shimmering stillness. An unspeakable face issued gently from the chalky wall—a dying youth—beauty of a homebent generation. The coolness of stones, moon-white, encircled the waking temple, the tread of shadows became inaudible on fallen steps, a rosy dance in the tiny garden.

Silent, I sat in an abandoned tavern, beneath incinerated beams, solitary adjacent my wine; a glowing corpse stooped over something dark and set a dead lamb at my feet. From putrefying blueness the sister's pale presence took form and her bloody mouth spoke: Sting, black thorn! And even now—O sadness—these silver arms resound from untamed storms. Flow, blood, from the moonish feet blossoming on the nighttime pathway across which a crying rat scurries. Flare up, you stars in my arching brow—and softly sounds the heart in the night. A red shadow stormed the house with a fiery sword, fled with a snowy brow: O bitter death.

And a dark voice spoke from within me: I broke my stallion's neck in the night wood because madness flared from his purple eyes; the shadows of elms fell upon me, a spring's blue laughter and the refreshing black coolness of night when I, a savage huntsman, roused the snowy beast: in stony hell my face was yielded to nothingness.

And, casting a faint glow, a drop of blood fell into the isolate wine, and when I drank its taste was more bitter than that of the poppy; and a blackish cloud enveloped my head, the crystal tears of fallen angels; and blood flowed gently from the sister's silver wound and a fiery rain fell on me.

I want to go along the edge of forests as one silenced, one from whose speechless hands the hair-shrouded sun sank, a stranger on the evening hill who, in tears, raises his eyelids over the stony town, something savage that stands calmly in the peace of aged elderberry trees: how restlessly the half-darkened head listens, or the hesitant steps of blue clouds follow to the hill, earnest constellations also. The green seed, calm, leads to the side—a shy deer attends on mossy forest ways. The huts of the villagers have been muted shut and in black tranquility the torrent's blue complaint becomes frightening.

But then I climbed down the rocky path and madness seized me and I cried out, loud in the night, and when, with silvery fingers, I bowed over the silent water, I saw my face had abandoned me. And the white voice spoke to me: Kill yourself! Sighing, a shadow child raised himself up within me and gazed at me radiant from crystal eyes so that, in tears, I sank down beneath the trees, beneath the forceful starry vault.

Unquiet wanderings across barbarous stone, far from evening towns, returning herds; distant, the setting sun grazes in a crystal meadow and her unshackled song ruffles, direly, the lonely cry of birds dying away in blue stillness. But you come softly in the night when, wakening, I lay on the hill, or else raging in spring's thunder storm; and yet more blackly, melancholy enclouds the secluded head, horrible lightning flashes frighten the nocturnal soul, your hands rip apart my unbreathing chest.

When I passed into the shadowy garden and the black complex of evil had moved away from me, the hyacinthine stillness of the night surrounded me, and I passed over the quiet pond in a curved boat and sweet peace touched my petrified brow. Speechless I lay beneath old willows and high above me was the sky, blue and filled with stars; and there, gazing on, I faded away, a mouldering—deep within me fear and pain died away, and the blue shadow of the boy lifted itself up radiant in the darkness, a gentle song; risen on moonish wings over the greening treetops: the crystal cliffs of the sister's white face.

With silver soles I climbed down the thorny steps and entered the white-washed chamber. A light burned quietly within and, in silence, I concealed my head in purple linen; and the earth cast up a child-like corpse, a lunar form that gradually became distinct from my shadow and fell down the stony precipice with broken arms, flocculent snow.

LETTERS

Translated
and annotated by

Siegfried Mandel

SECONDS BEFORE ETERNITY

Siegfried Mandel

"Forgive this grating eccentric who would rather slip into a peasant's skin than make verses in the sweat of his face," wrote Georg Trakl in a letter to Irene Amtmann, one of his few women acquaintances. A wealth of personal meanings is encapsuled in such frank declarations: the knowledge of himself, his predilection for the interior life, the agony of composition and the necessity of its pain—as in the myth of Adam expelled from Paradise and ordained by God "to toil in the sweat of his face." He lived the myth in its literal dimensions: toilsome work, the breaking of tabus, the fall into a life of self-punishing torment as real as depictions by Dostoevsky, the lodestar for Trakl's sufferings. If the letters have qualities far from the aesthetic, they reflect Trakl's disinclination to elevate private torment into pleasing forms. "One does well," Trakl also wrote to Miss Irene Amtmann, the catalyst for his self-observations, "to resist completed beauty in the face of which nothing remains except one's imbecilic viewing. No, the solution for someone like myself consists of going forward to one's self!" Completed beauty and contemplation of it were of no interest to Trakl. He was drawn to figures living at the margins of society and in the darkness of tabus to which he had himself succumbed. The "going forward to one's self"—one's fate or destiny as Trakl pessimistically felt—is recorded in the poetry, the prose-poems, the closet dramas, and the surviving correspondence from 1905 to 1914. Written a week before his suicide, Trakl's last letters contain a brief testament and several poems which in title and substance told of lament and human misery—not only his own—which he had fully tasted during his short life and finally on the battlefield.

Letters are attuned most often, of course, to the personality and status of their recipients and to the needs of the writer. Trakl's financial support came from his family but could not keep pace with his relentless spendings. In the wake of much joblessness, caused by an inability to accommodate himself to steady contact with people and workaday chores, many letters contain pleas for money and loans, negotiations for publication of poems and books, and other mundane matters that helped to keep him afloat. Lodgings, drugs and drink created incessant monetary demands. Publication of poetry brought little remuneration, while book publication and advances depended to an extent upon subscribers' lists which Trakl and his friends were to provide. In placing some of his work, Trakl was fortunate to have the encouragement and advice of two friends—Erhard Buschbeck and Ludwig von Ficker—who knew the ways of publicity and business. The 20-year-old Buschbeck outlined certain strategies in his letters to Trakl: Since every editor consults Kürschner's literary calendar, why not write to him ("the deflowerer of virgin poets") and "really make some publicity for yourself." Neither the publicizing nor merchandising of poetry would have found Trakl able to cope on his own. For Trakl, poverty was neither genteel nor ennobling. Invariably, he shut out poverty by yielding to it and allowing it—along with prodigious bouts of drink and drugs—to become a stimulus for incurably obsessive self-punishing phantasies that inform his life and works.

Trakl could not relax into a leisurely tempo of correspondence or philosophical expositions and ruminations. The earliest letters tried to reach out and establish continuing contacts, but rapidly they became eruptions—terse, cryptic cries and statements, or formal necessities. He did not cultivate or regard letters—the way Rilke did—as part of his oeuvre or as a means for contemporaries and posterity to understand and interpret either his person or his poetry. Yet they succeed naturally in illuminating the relationships among life, thought, and work.

Trakl's letters contain no ounce of literate pretentiousness, preciosity or affectation; he wrote without a mask and abjured conscious role playing. The way Trakl generally wrote was the way friends remembered his speaking, with pointedness and stunted force. When he did articulate the poetic drive, he illuminated the truth of a reality that transcended the boundaries of life. The other-earthliness of his visions were forged in the living hell, as he put it, "of all the animalistic drives that roll life through time." What his poetry suggests implicitly, his letters say with eloquent, explicit ruggedness. Of the letters, the greatest losses are those between himself and his younger sister Margarethe (Gretl or Grete as Georg addressed her). One suspects that a censorious hand destroyed them, for the letters mirrored the transgression and phantasies of two accomplices—uncommonly gifted in the arts and dangerously close psychologically—in a nightmare of incest; they drifted in the backwash of their guilt. In Grete's copy of Gustave Flaubert's *Madame Bovary: Ein Sittenbild aus der Provinz*, Trakl wrote the following dedication: "To my beloved little demon who arose from the sweetest and deepest fables of the 1001 Nights....In Memoriam! Salzburg, summer of 1908." She was also the threatening and "flaming demon" in the prose-poem "Traum and Um-nachtung"* ("Dream and Derangement"), the "dark melody" of his life and poetry; she appears variously as a dionysic saint or an androgynous "female monk," a youthful Virgin Mary with a moon's halo, as a mirror-image of himself, or in his last poem, "Grodek,"* as a shadowy figure who greets the spirits of the fallen "heroes" (not victims). For the most part of their lives, from childhood on, Georg and Grete idolized each other.

As for the extant communications, we have some 140 letters, notes, postcards, and telegrams. These not only deepen our perspectives of Trakl's biography and creativity but unify them dramatically. In the excerpts and selections here, we find unsparing self-portraiture, recurrent images and symbols wrought in Trakl's inner smithy, the maturing intentionality of poetic aims and techniques, an unmediated view of experience, as well as the anguished sensibility and unedited thoughts that constitute the disturbed and conflicted personality of the poet and person. He survived the great "enmity of life," defied and struggled with it, and finally found it intolerable.

One might wish that Trakl had consistently written aphorisms which voiced his running reflections. Only two remain and are six years apart in his compressed life. One is a rationalization of the twenty-year old and the other a summing up by a prematurely aged person in the year of his death:

(Aphorism I) Only to one who despises happiness comes enlightenment.
(Inscribed on a photo, March 18, 1908.)

(Aphorism II) The sensation in moments of deathlike being: All humans are worthy of love. Awakening, you feel the world's bitterness; in that lies all your unresolved guilt; your poem is incomplete atonement.
(Probably August 24, 1914.)

This latter aphorism appeared in the form of a note handed by Trakl to Ludwig von Ficker, who regarded it as a personal "orientation" or explanation, silent and meaningful. When Ficker looked up questioningly from the note, Trakl added, "But, of course, no poem ever can be atonement for guilt."

---

* This symbol indicates that the work is translated in this volume.

Salzburg, August/mid-September 1905 (?)

...Vacation has begun as badly for me as possible. For eight days I have been ill—in a desperate mood. At first I worked much, yes, very much [on Gymnasium make-up examinations]. To get over the lingering tensions after nervous relief, I regrettably again took refuge in chloroform. The effect was horrible. For eight days now I have suffered from it—my nerves are frazzled. But I am resisting the temptation to calm myself again through such means because I see catastrophe too close at hand....
(To Karl von Kalmár in Vienna.)

Except for superior grades in physical education, Trakl's lack of concentration, dreamy "spinning," and stoic indifference earned him failures in academic studies. He did not return to his Gymnasium schooling and instead began an apprenticeship in a pharmacy called "Zum weissen Engel," a curious but not unsymbolic name—The White Angel. Although Trakl had been in the habit of carrying a flask of chloroform, no one took seriously his attention-getting declarations that death in etherized throes must be wonderful, or his raptures about the incest motif in Wagner's *Die Walküre*. Kalmár was a Gymnasium classmate, and occasionally hosted the lonely Trakl when he was in Vienna.

Salzburg, September 30, 1906

...You know, dear friend, that I can communicate best with others through the written word. I have never had the gift of speaking. And so I think it would be best to send you a small token of my recent work. Perhaps you can read in it what is not possible for me to say so readily. This year I worked very, very little. Completed only short stories. The road ahead seems to me to become more and more difficult! All the better for that!...
(To Karl von Kalmár in Vienna.)

Vienna, October 5, 1908

...What happened to me these days interested me sufficiently to make me observant because, everything taken into account, things appeared uncommon and yet not exceptional. When I arrived here, it seemed as if for the first time I saw life as clear as it is, without subjective interpretations—naked and without preconceptions—as if I perceived all those voices expressed by reality, gruesome and painfully perceivable. And for a moment I sense something of the pressure that ordinarily burdens people and sense the driving force of fate.

I believe that it must be terrible always to live like this in the full emotion of all the animalistic drives that roll life through time. The most terrible possibilities have I felt, smelled, groped at within me, and have heard the demons howl in my blood—the thousand devils whose stings drive one's flesh mad. What a shocking nightmare!

Gone! Today that vision of reality has sunk again into nothingness—distant from me are objects and even more distant yet their voices, and I listen again with an inspired ear to the melodies that are within me, and my winged eye again dreams its pictures which are more beautiful than all of reality! I am at home with myself and am my world! My total, beautiful world full of infinite euphony....

(To Hermine Aurelia von Rauterberg, Trakl's sister "Minna," three years older than Georg; she was married to a railway official in Salzburg.)

If this letter has been seen as the crystallization of a neurosis and a desperate aim to repress drives and fears, it also reflects a specific stage in Trakl's work when a lyrical mode of musical composition of poetry by ear was dominant. Suggested is the lulling and druglike effect of poetic listening and escape into words as the poet is repelled by reality. Opposites abound: dream and nightmare, visions of reality and waking reality; Trakl's eye dreams and creates pictures more beautiful than reality; the instinctual life maddens the conscious flesh. The reassuring harmony of words that are substitutes for reality becomes almost programmatic. Such euphoria wears off later, however, and while the themes remain constant, Trakl's techniques change drastically.

Vienna, end of October, 1908

...Every line, every letter which arrives from Salzburg is one of my heart's dearest remembrances of a city which I love above all, and a remembrance of the few to whom my love belongs.

I would think that the Kapuzinerberg has already risen in the fiery red of autumn and the Gaisberg has clothed itself in a soft gown best suited to its trim lines. The glockenspiel plays "the last rose...," blending into the serious, friendly evening, so sweetly moving that the heavens arch into infinity! And the fountain's song wafts so melodically over the Residenzplatz, and the Dom throws majestic shadows. And the silence rises and wanders over plazas and streets. If I could linger with you in the midst of all that splendor, things would be better for me. I don't know if anyone else can feel the magic of that city as I can, a magic that saddens one's heart with excessive happiness. I am always sad when I am happy! Isn't that strange!

I don't like the Viennese at all. Here is a citizenry that hides uncountable dumb, silly, and even mean characteristics behind an unpleasant bonhomie. Nothing is more distasteful to me than a sham emphasis on Gemütlichkeit! On the trolley the conductor treats one too familiarly, likewise the waiters at the inn, etc. Everyone is parasitically assaulted [angestrudelt] in the most shameless way. And the end-goal of all these outrages is—the tip! I have already had to make the discovery that in Vienna everything has its tax-tip. The devil take these shameless bedbugs!...
(To Maria Geipel in Salzburg, called "Mitzie" by the family and "dear little sister" by Georg who was four years younger.)

Poetically and physically Trakl felt drawn to the breath of autumn in which life flares up and decays, and "wide open are the chambers of death and beautifully painted by sunshine." The opening line of the poem "An meine Schwester"* ("To my Sister") reads: "Where you walk, there it is autumn and evening." The thronged and stony cities of Austria caused strong and mixed reactions in Trakl, usually in proportion to his closeness or distance from them. Occasional soft words for Salzburg were outweighed by tirades and metrophobia. He found unsolicited contacts physically repellent and unbearable intrusions into his privacy; the impoverishment and grinding cold of his lodgings exacerbated his discomfort; the superficial glitter of Viennese waltzes, lyric tenors, whipped-cream gluttony and the hostility to intellectuals created an atmosphere of decay that merited not one line of admiration in his works but words of condemnation in his letters for the reactionary treatment of creative people as court clowns or disposable cynics. When asked why he did not choose to live in the countryside instead, Trakl brusquely answered, "I have no right to withdraw from hell." The phrase is drawn verbatim from

Dostoevsky's novel *The Idiot.*

Vienna, June 11, 1909

You cannot readily imagine the delight when one is transported...when everything which has streamed toward one during the past year and has painfully demanded release and so suddenly and unexpectedly storms into the light—released and releasing. I have blessed days behind me—oh would that there be even richer ones ahead without end, so that I can render and return what I have received—and to experience it as anyone else might who could endure it.

  That would be the life!
(To Erhard Buschbeck in Salzburg.)

From school days on Buschbeck was Trakl's intimate friend and voluntary, unofficial literary agent. With this letter, Trakl sent poems grouped under the title *Aus goldenem Kelch (From the Golden Cup)* for which Buschbeck found no publisher until 1939, twenty-five years after the poet's death. Among the poems is "Blutschuld" (Blood-Guilt), which Ernst Günther Bleisch, in his study *Georg Trakl*, characterizes as the only genuine love poem in Trakl's oeuvre:

> Night threatens at the bedside of our kisses.
> There is a whisper: Who lifts the guilt from you?
> Still quivering from damned lecher's sweetness
> We pray: Forgive us, Maria, in your grace!
>
> From flower cups rise greedy aromas,
> Flattering our brows white with guilt.
> Exhausted under the breath of oppressive airs
> We dream: Forgive us, Maria, in your grace!
>
> Yet, louder roars the fountain of sirens
> And more darkly the spinx rears up before our guilt,
> So that evermore sinful become our hearts' sounds,
> We sob: Forgive us, Maria, in your grace!

Trakl and his sister, Grete, could not cope with their early incest compulsions, and during puberty they thought of suicide; when separated later, they carried their tormenting guilt with them to the end of their tragic lives. In recurrent lines of his poems, and particularly in the hellish prose poem "Traum und Umnachtung* ("Dream and Derangement"), incest is relived. Maria at one and the same time is the actual mother of Georg and Grete, who censoriously haunts the sibling-lovers and is the divinity who sees all and forgives. A literary undercurrent played upon is Goethe's Faust-and-Gretchen seduction-scenario. A reticent partner in the life-drama, Buschbeck is bound psychologically in subterranean fashion to Trakl through a brief, dramatic affair with Grete in 1912; it is conjectured that Georg only became aware of this much later, but I suspect that while the poet intuitively deflected that knowledge into his prose poems and dramas, the person stonily suppressed it.

Salzburg, October (?), 1909

...I thank you heartily for the kind contact with Hermann Bahr...which for the first time makes my poems accessible to a significant critic, no matter what his judgment might be....All that I hope from him is that his reasoned and self-assured criticism will anchor and clarify my perennially wobbling nature that is desperate about everything....
(To Erhard Buschbeck, in Vienna.)

Bahr assisted Trakl's debut in the widely-read *Neue Wiener Journal*, a Viennese daily; on October 17, 1909, the newspaper published three of Trakl's poems. The critic, whose tastes were generally lampooned as Viennese "Bahroque," rapidly lost interest in Trakl. Grete never forgave Bahr and acidly she wrote to Buschbeck, who was to become Bahr's secretary at the court theatre: "About your friend Bahr, you will no doubt also hear news from other sources. To my chagrin he makes all churches here unsafe; already at 7:30 a.m. he slides around the Pfarrkirche [Salzburg] on his knees. One could have a spitting fit."

Vienna, between August 9-15, 1910

...Stood two examinations [for a pharmacy degree at the University]....I am all alone in Vienna. Endure it nevertheless! ...I am inclined to enshroud myself and otherwise become invisible. And one always is thrown back upon words or, better expressed, upon

94

terrible helplessness....Probably I will come home...am not happy about that....
(To Erhard Buschbeck in Salzburg.)

Vienna, second half of July, 1910

...I must tell you about an incident which has affected me painfully.
Yesterday Mr. [Ludwig] Ullman explained that many of his concerns matched mine, and he read a poem to me....What appeared was more than affinity with my poem "Der Gewitterabend." Not only were the individual images and turns of phrase taken over almost verbatim but also the rhyme and stress... as well as my picturelike manner which in four stanza lines melds four separate parts of a picture into a single impression....Even if this "related" poem lacks the living fever which must seek its form precisely, and even if it is makeshift and without a soul, it cannot be a matter of indifference to me, here or elsewhere, to see a distorted picture of my own face as mask in front of a stranger's face....Truly, the idea of it fills me with loathing....
(To Erhard Buschbeck in Salzburg.)

Vienna, second half of July, 1910

...it already is completely immaterial to me. What does it matter if someone finds it of worth to imitate my work. That he must square with his own conscience.
That Mr. Ullmann has recommended my work to Stefan Zweig is something I thank him for!...
Recently I have been harrassed by too much (what an infernal chaos of rhythms and images), so that I had little time for things other than to shape these in some small measure in order not to appear as a silly bungler—reduced to cramps and delirium by the slightest external jolt—in the face of what one cannot conquer.
I have written to Karl Kraus, quite impersonally and coldly, and will probably not expect much from him....
(To Erhard Buschbeck in Salzburg.)

Ludwig Ullman (1887-1959) was a free-lance journalist, on the board of the periodical *Der Ruf*, and a playwright and drama critic in Vienna. He and his wife (the former Irene Amtmann) became reliable friends of Trakl. Further, the poet's fears expressed in his letter proved unfounded when the formidable cultural gadfly Karl Kraus (1874-1936) and editor of *Die Fackel* greeted Trakl's work with respect and enthusiasm. Trakl was to draw strength from Kraus' fearless ideological work, and with admiration he dedicated several poems to Kraus.

Vienna, Autumn, 1910

...and so I sit through the year and find it regrettable that in such matters my "popo" is the only thing that is exercised....Mitzi seems to be comfortable in Switzerland, and Gretl...from time to time sends me eccentric epistles.

From home, as usual, I have no news. Recently I changed my residence and am housed in a room no larger than a water closet....Privately I fear turning idiotic in it. I look out at a small, dark yard. When one looks out of the window, one can turn to stone with disconsolation....

(To Friedrich or "Fritz" Trakl, in Rovereto, Italy. Trakl's younger brother served as an Austrian army officer.)

Salzburg, early Autumn, 1910 or 1911

Dear Miss! [Irene Amtmann]

It seems to me that I wander around daily like a vagabond, at times in the forests which already are very reddish and airy and where hunters now harrass the wild life to death, or I wander in streets within disconsolate and bleak sections, or lounge around Salzach and watch the seagulls (that is still my happiest lazing). But there is more unrest in me than I would want to admit, and so your friendly letter has long and in unseemly fashion lain unreciprocated. Forgive this grating eccentric who would rather slip into a peasant's skin than make verses in the sweat of his face. Need I say that I am more than impatient to return to Vienna where I can belong to myself, something that is not granted me here.

One can scold me perhaps as being ungrateful under this wonderful, pure sky of the homeland, so to speak, but one does well to resist completed beauty in the face of which nothing remains except one's imbecilic viewing. No, the solution for someone like myself consists of going forward to one's self! At

times, however, one grants oneself leisure in order at least to answer charming letters amicably.
(To Irene Amtmann in Vienna.)

Trakl met the young lady in 1910, along with Ludwig Ullmann who was to become her husband. In this uninhibited letter, Trakl describes his state of mind and absorptions; of particular interest are the statements that reject pure estheticism. One of Amtmann's surviving letters to Trakl suggests that she kept up with his poetry and often tried to humor him out of his despondencies.

Vienna, May 20, 1911

[Dr. Franz] Schwab was in Vienna for 14 days and—as wildly as never before—we wined, dined, and caroused throughout the nights. I believe that both of us were completely crazy....
(To Erhard Buschbeck in Salzburg.)

Schwab was an old school friend. There is no exaggeration in Trakl's letter since he was capable alone or in the company of friends like Schwab and Karl Minnich, both from Salzburg, of prodigious drinking bouts. Some friends claimed that these bouts neither diminished Trakl's clarity nor inhibited his poetizing. One thing is certain: Trakl's physical constitution, which allowed him to excel in physical education during school days, was rugged until worn down by enormous fatigue.

Vienna, June 27, 1911

... My sister has already inquired several times about your address, and I fear that she will ask you for the copy of the writings that I once left with you during an attack of thoughtlessness; heavens only knows what phantastic projects she will attempt to undertake with them. I beg you not to release anything, since I cannot tolerate something being undertaken without my consent and for which I have not considered the time ripe.
   Best of all, in any case, would be to return those damned manuscripts to me. You could do me no greater favor....
(To Erhard Buschbeck in Salzburg.)

Salzburg, November 13, 1911

From beautiful Salzburg, best greetings (signed, Karl [Minnich]).

When a little Jew fucks, he gets winged lice! A baptized Christian hears all the angels sing [signed G. T. and followed by some text by Karl Hauer].
(A joint postcard to Erhard Buschbeck in Vienna.)

Trakl's biographer Otto Basil points to other sometimes "pornographic or anti-Semitic volleys from his hand." Anti-Semitism achieved epidemic proportions among Austrian political and social stratas, ranging from deliberate anti-liberal strategies to chic or thoughtless prejudices among much of the population. Although Trakl, an Evangelical Protestant, had many helpful Jewish acquaintances, others of his friends were not untainted by anti-Semitism. Grete, for one, never gave up her prejudices. Basil suggests that Trakl was to purge puerile thoughtlessness in correspondences and life:

> Later with the final form of Trakl's poetry and a concurrent full maturity, he was to despise obscenities; it was impossible in his presence to make a slippery observation, and of women—even the purchasable ones—he always spoke with high regard and even with tributes.

Other sources tell us that Trakl regarded "racial differences" as "incidentals."
"Afra" and "Sonja" are poems that derive from the mature attitudes described by Basil, and they mirror a self-stylization derived as well from the fictive features of Dostoevskian figures and the life modes of Baudelaire and Rimbaud:

AFRA

A child with brown hair. Prayer and acquiescence
Softly darken the evening-like coolness
And Afra's smile, red in a yellow frame
Of sunflowers, fear and the stiflings of grey heat.

The monk saw her in a previous time, cloaked
In a blue shawl, a pious image in church windows;
This will still be a kind escort in sorrow
When their stars race spectral through his blood.

Autumn decline; and a silence of elderberries.
The forehead touches the water's blue stirrings,
A sack-cloth shroud laid over a bier.

Rotted fruits fall from the branches;
Unspeakable is the bird's flight, this meeting
With the dying; and dark years follow.

(tr. Roderick Iverson)

SONJA

Evening spills to the old garden;
Sonja's life, a bluish stillness.
Wild birds traversing distance;
A barren tree in autumn, stillness.

A sunflower, gently bowed
Over Sonja's white life.
The wound, red and hidden,
Is permitted life in dark rooms

Where blue bells tone;
Sonja's step and gentle stillness.
The dying animal greets in passing,
Barren tree in autumn, stillness.

A sun of ancient days shines
Above Sonja's white brow,
Snow that moistens her cheeks,
And the wilderness of her brow.

(tr. Roderick Iverson)

Sonja's life, like Trakl's own, in the poem consists of blue stillness or silence, and Sonja possesses a wound "red and hidden." During Trakl's student days in Salzburg, his bordello-visits with boon companions were frequent. Certainly, his reported predilection for sitting with a withered, old whore, drinking wine and spinning monologues seems like something invented by Dostoevsky. Trakl's complex personality is defined by voyeuristic and aggressive tendencies, identification with women of humble status and profession (the humiliated), his anti-bourgeois sentiments, rebellion against the closeted-atmosphere of his family home, and the willful breaking of tabus. The "only woman of erotic dominance," in Basil's phrase, was his sister Grete.

Karl Hauer, who shares the postcard written to Buschbeck, met Trakl in the circle of the Pan Society of Literature and Art in Salzburg; Hauer was twelve years older than Trakl. Like Verlaine and Rimbaud, Trakl and Hauer were boon companions to excess and their social backgrounds were similar. A brilliant polemical and anarchic essayist, Hauer also knew many people in the arts and helped Trakl make social and literary contacts, particularly with the controversial architect Alfred Loos and the feared political journalist Karl Kraus.

Salzburg (?), late Autumn (?), 1911

Enclosed is the revised poem ["Klagelied," "Lamentation"]. It is that much better than the original because it now is impersonal and bursts with movement and is filled with visions.

I am convinced that in this universal form and manner it will mean and say more than in the limited personal way of the first version.

You may well believe me that it does not come easy, nor ever will it, to subordinate myself unconditionally to that which is to be recorded, and I will always and always need to correct myself in order to give truth its due.

(To Erhard Buschbeck, probably in Vienna.)

"Klagelied," a lament over the children murdered by King Herod, is not a memorable poem and cannot be contrasted with the earlier version which is lost. But the letter contains a significant statement of intentions, which clarified for Trakl a new direction and theory of poetic work: a change in techniques had to accompany that theory. A transition had to be made from poems that were essentially descriptive, that followed conventions of metrical forms, that relied on subjective renditions of concrete images whose relationships were readily discernible, and that appealed to the ear through musicality. The newer poetry for Trakl avoided personal comment and gained objective truth through images that are abstracted from the concrete—images which themselves became the key events; declamations, "reporting," and free verse were to be mastered.

Critics have noted that Trakl's poetry shifted also from a gentle melancholy to a gentle madness indicated by harsher imagery. Equally noteworthy in the letter is the clue to Trakl's ceaseless revisions and retractions. Apparently, he had a compulsive need to correct himself in seeking to render truth.

Salzburg, possibly end of January, 1912

...a few rhythms from my inferno. Greet Schwab who, as I found out from Minnich in Vienna, drinks a more joyous wine in Salzburg....

How long must I meander in the cursed city?...I sit and burn with impatience and with rages against myself. Fate seems to me idiotic in that it does not make better use of me....In sad boredom. Your G.T.
(To Erhard Buschbeck in Vienna.)

Innsbruck, before April 21, 1912

...I never would have believed that I would have to pass my life, during an already difficult time, in the most brutal and mean city that exists in this burdened and cursed world. And when I think further that an alien will has caused me to suffer here for about a decade, then I could succumb to a crying fit of inconsolable helplessness.

Why torture myself. For ultimately I shall always remain a poor Caspar Hauser.
(To Erhard Buschbeck in Vienna.)

At the time Trakl wrote this letter he was in the service of the garrison hospital's pharmacy and lived in Pradl, a depressing section near the Innsbruck railroad station. Life in the stony cities of the plains posed the same problem for Trakl as it had for Caspar Hauser. Other similarities reside in their problematic childhoods, the attraction to cemeteries and necrophilic sensations, the in-capability of adapting to and dealing with the practical world, and the love of nature and landscape (which in Trakl's poetry became a self-identifying immersion). In his "Caspar Hauser"* poem published in November 1913, Trakl projected the feeling of being "alone with his star" and yearned for the "blue cave" of his childhood (as in his poem "Kindheit"). Caspar Hauser merged with another figure in Trakl's mind—one who could speak no language until he was twenty—namely, Dostoevsky's Prince Myschkin in *The Idiot*. Trakl needed desperately to define himself between the extremes of the saintly and the demoniacal. He felt that he had the same gift as the "idiot" Myschkin to see more clearly than the so-called normal run of humans but had to suffer ridicule and the designation of being a crazy person, according to Trakl's sister 'Mitzie' who in August 1965 told this to Gottfried Stix, the author of *Trakl und Wassermann*.

Innsbruck, April 24, 1912

...I do not believe that I will find anyone here to my liking, and the city and its environs—I am sure of it—grow ever more repulsive....Perhaps though, I'll go to Borneo. Somewhere the storm that gathers within me will yet discharge itself, for my and my heart's sake, even through sickness and melancholy.

At any rate, I am bearing all this distraughtness somewhat cheerfully and not altogether unvocally....
(To Erhard Buschbeck in Vienna.)

Soon after this letter, Trakl was introduced to Ludwig von Ficker (editor of the reputable semi-monthly *Der Brenner*) who had begun to publish Trakl's poems. The publication became the steadiest periodical-outlet for Trakl, while Ficker willingly eased into the role of a most sympathetic father-figure. Trakl's visionary, apocalyptic poetry found a congenial place in the religio-philosophical communality of *Der Brenner* and its circle, which also understood sexual morality to be entwined with a religious heritage. Ficker was attracted to the imposing, dark eccentricities of Trakl.

Innsbruck, mid-October, 1912

...Hope: 100 camels who will subscribe! 50 percent! Say! fifty%!

Oh that Buschbeck and his poet=two (write) 2 holy (ho-ly) fools.
....Vonwiller: a laughing philosopher! Oh sleep! The wine was superb, the cigarettes excellent, the mood dionysic, and the trip completely crappy; the morning shameless, fevered, the head full of pain, damnation and afflicted jugglery!

It was so cold that my insides are frozen. 'Fraud' heated room, and a comfortableness that lets hemorrhoids grow in one's arse....

Do not forget, all-powerful-one, to make conscientiously the corrections for the poem "Drei Blicke in einen Opal"....
(To Erhard Buschbeck in Vienna.)

To help subsidize publication in 1913 of Trakl's first volume of poems by the Kurt Wolff Verlag in Leipzig, advance subscribers had to be solicited. The Oskar Vonwiller mentioned was a friend dating back to school days. He had also been a part of the Brenner circle which was to make Trakl's stay in Innsbruck more endurable, although in December 1912 he wrote of Innsbruck as this "long-dead city." In many of the letters addressed to Buschbeck, Trakl also hovered over his poems like a brooding hen.

Innsbruck, about October, 1912

...Much light, much warmth and a quiet strip of beach on which to live and I would need no more than that to become a beautiful angel. At any rate, one plays a bad joke upon oneself by becoming a military pharmacist assistant....
(To Ludwig Ullman in Vienna.)

In the next letter—to Buschbeck—Trakl mentions the bitter cold of Innsbruck and the "evening of red wine-heating," a 4 a.m. frost bath in moonlight on the balcony, and writing a "magnificent" poem that skitters with the cold.

Innsbruck, January 4, 1913

Like a dead soul I travelled past Hall, a black city that plunged right through me like an inferno through a damned one.

In Mühlau I went through sheer sunlight and am still staggering. Veronal has granted me some sleep under Kokoschka's Franziska.

I'll linger as long as possible. Please send me my travel bag since I need some essential laundry.

Please write, dear friend, if my mother has much worry on my account....

(To Erhard Buschbeck in Salzburg, written on a postcard with the address of the editorial office of *Der Brenner* at Innsbruck-Mühlau.)

A few references to Oskar Kokoschka appear in Trakl letters. Among the Viennese intellectuals Trakl met in cafés and favorite drinking places, the free-wheeling journalist Karl Kraus, the avant-garde architect Adolf Loos (whose buildings created considerable controversy), and the expressionist painter Kokoschka were the few of lasting interest in European cultural history. Kokoschka's *Franziska* mentioned by Trakl might be a reproduction of a painting that since then may have been given another title. In the fall of 1912, Kokoschka rented a studio near the Prater. Kokoschka, like Trakl, had been wrestling with new forms of expression that would translate his emotions into pictorial shapes during a difficult phase of his life. On his canvas was a work in progress called *Windsbraut (Tempest)* that portrays two figures reclining in a floating boat. The woman tranquilly reposes on the man's chest, while he wears an alert expression of passion, weary fatefulness and quiet despair. "Windsbraut" not only means tempest but also poetically "bride of the wind." Trakl was entranced, and Kokoschka wrote of his frequent visits:

> Surely, together we painted the *Windsbraut*; I also saw one of his self-portraits. At the time I painted the *Windsbraut*, he was with me daily. I had a very primitive studio and he sat behind me mutely on a beer barrel. Sometimes he began to speak in a droning voice and without pause. Then he remained silent for hours on end. Both of us at the time were societal miscreants. I had left my parental home; storms were unloaded on my exhibitions and art. At any rate, Trakl put the *Windsbraut* into his poetry *verbatim*.

Kokoschka had in mind the poem "Die Nacht"*("Night"), published in 1914/15 in *Der Brenner*, which interprets rather than describes the painting.

Trakl's mother, at the time he expressed worry in this letter, had been a widow for two-and-a-half years. She was the figure-head for the Tobias Trakl and Co. hardware business, while other members, including a son by a previous marriage, took care of its management. Georg received periodic subsidies, which rarely satisfied his wants. From the start of her marriage, Maria Trakl had lived in a shell within the family. She was protected by her collection of antiques. At the same time, her eccentric ways, including drug addiction, clashed with her husband's strict and patriarchal air and benevolence. In the poem "Geburt"* ("Birth"), she is a terrifying and silent figure. The parental contrast is even sharper in "Sebastian im Traum"* ("Sebastian in Dream"). Within "Sebastian" we see the boy crossing the autumnal Salzburg cemetery, held by the freezing hand of the mother, while another image shows him holding the reassuring hand of his father. When Trakl lost his father in June of 1910, he also lost one of the few potentially stabilizing forces in his emotional maelstrom.

Innsbruck, after mid-January, 1913

...In the next few days, I will send you a proof sheet of "Helian." It is the most precious and painful poem I have ever written.... (To Erhard Buschbeck in Vienna.)

"Helian"* was published in February, 1913, in *Der Brenner*.

Salzburg, beginning February, 1913

...Regrettably, I cannot move to Eugendorf, as I had planned, since events have occurred in regard to my mother that require dissolving of business and household in Salzburg. Amid this bitterness and worry about the near future, it would seem to me frivolous to leave my mother's house. In the event that I return to military service, I would like to ask you to write to Mr. Robert Michel to see if he can help to arrange my transfer to Vienna or, again, to Innsbruck.... (To Ludwig von Ficker in Innsbruck.)

Salzburg, about February 19, 1913

...I do not have easy days at home now and I drift between fever and helplessness in sunny rooms where it is unspeakably cold.

Strange shudders of transformation, bodily experienced to the point of unbearability; visions of mysteries until the certainty of having died; ecstasies to the point of stony petrifaction; and a continuation of dreaming sad dreams. How dark is this moldy city, full of churches and pictures of death.
(To Karl Borromaeus Heinrich in Innsbruck.)

An essayist and novelist, Heinrich befriended Trakl within the Brenner circle. A month after the appearance of "Helian," Heinrich wrote an appreciative article on Trakl in the same journal. Heinrich used as his text the apocalyptic visions of the West's decline as limned in "Helian." The images and emotions of a pseudo-death in the letter typify those in the poetry.

Salzburg, February 23, 1913

For your kind letter, I give most heartfelt thanks. Ever more deeply do I feel what the Brenner means to me—home and shelter within the circle of a noble humaneness. Am afflicted by indescribably shattering events, and I do not know if they will destroy or perfect me. I despair at everything I begin, and in the face of a ridiculously uncertain future, I feel more deeply than I can express the happiness given by your generosity and the compassionate understanding of your friendship.

It frightens me how in recent times an unexplainable hatred against me has multiplied and which appears with grotesque distortions in the smallest incidents in my daily life. My stay here is disagreeable to a point of surfeit, without my having the strength to decide upon leaving.

Enclosed is the new version of a poem ["Untergang"* ("Decline")] dedicated to Dr. Heinrich, for which I request publication in the next issue of *Der Brenner*. The first version contains something only hinted at.
(To Ludwig von Ficker in Innsbruck.)

Relationships were strained at a family reunion during the pressures of dissolving the Trakl family business, and Georg's concern for his financial situation was evident. Trakl turned increasingly to Ficker—rather than the family friend Buschbeck—with his personal troubles, and Ficker invariably lent a sympathetic ear. "Untergang"* ("Decline"), the poem men-

106

tioned by Trakl, was actually the fifth revision of the original. In subsequent letters, no matter what his mood, Trakl concerned himself with revisions of older poems to bring them into line with his perception of how a poem ought to be written currently, though retaining the essential theme of an earlier version. Businesslike letters also went to his new book publisher Kurt Wolff, indicating his own preferences for the manner of production for his poetry. Ficker advised him in his business dealings. Heinrich of the Brenner circle—to whom the mentioned poem was dedicated—had suicidal tendencies and caused Trakl and others great concern.

Salzburg, June 26, 1913

...Here, one day is more overcast and colder than the next and it rains without let-up. Sometimes a ray of the last sunny days from Innsbruck falls into this darkness and fills me with deep thankfulness for you and all the noble people whose generosity, in truth, I do not at all deserve. Too little love; all too much hardness, arrogance, and assorted criminality—that is my self. I am certain that I forego wickedness only out of weakness and cowardice and thereby put my wickedness to shame. I long for the day when the soul neither will nor can live any longer in this unholy body made pestilent by melancholy, and that the soul will leave this absurd body composed of filth and decay—a body that is only an all-too-true mirror image of a godless and cursed century.

Oh God, only a small spark of pure joy—and one would be saved; love—and one would be freed....
(To Ludwig von Ficker in Innsbruck.)

Here are terrifying deprecations of the body, and the self-image supposedly is what Trakl saw in the mirror as he came out of a deep sleep at night. It is an incident caught also in the prose poem "Traum und Umnachtung"* ("Dream and Derangement"), in which the "cursed" siblings in the broken mirror are swallowed up by the night. In the studio of an artist-friend, Trakl once rapidly painted a gruesome death-in-life self-portrait, with blue-green and scarlet paint splotches surrounding the hollows of mouth and eyes. Such pathological eruptions and moods are reflected in some letters, alternating with wry cheerfulness as at the prospects of spending a rare vacation outside of Austria with friends. Heading for Venice, he declared in a postcard to Buschbeck (August 15,

1913): "...The world is round. Saturday I'll fall down into Venice. Ever farther—to the stars." Fears of falling and decline were ingrained in Trakl's anticipations. In a retrospective poem, he called Venice an antechamber of hell.

Vienna, November 11, 1913

...I slept through the last two days and nights and still have a real aggravating case of veronal poisoning. In my confusion and desperation in recent times, I now really don't know how I shall continue to live....

Dear Friend, would you please make the following corrections in the "Kaspar Hauser Lied"* ("Caspar Hauser Song")....
(To Ludwig von Ficker in Innsbruck.)

Vienna, November 17, 1913

Many thanks for your invitation to give a reading in Innsbruck. I can definitely accept it just as definitely as I cannot remain in Vienna, this garbage-city [Dreckstadt]. I will return to the military unconditionally, that is, if I still would be accepted. I hope that you can still arrange the dedication [of the "Caspar Hauser Song"]. I have already given [Adolf] Loos a copy of the poem which carried this dedication [to Loos' wife, Bessie], and Loos has shown it to many people. It would be painful to me therefore if the poem were to appear without the dedication, especially since Loos asked me for it....
(To Ludwig von Ficker.)

Trakl at times refused to allow his poems to be read at public performances, but on one occasion accepted an invitation to read under the sponsorship of the Brenner as mentioned in this letter. His feelings toward Vienna remained virtually unchanged. In regard to the army, he turned to it repeatedly for medical-pharmacy or desk positions, and just as readily sought to be discharged. Despite his avowed loathing for any kind of bureaucracy, he found temporary shelter there from responsibilities, just as in his poetry there are regressive flights into the "blue cave" of childhood. As for friends who tolerated his eccentricities, he often reciprocated with dedications of his poems.

Vienna, end of (?) November, 1913

...[Karl] Kraus sends you many greetings. Dr. Heinrich, here, once again has been taken seriously ill; and, in the past days quite terrible things have transpired, whose shadow I cannot shake off during my lifetime. Yes, dear friend, within the span of a few days events have broken up my life unspeakably, and what remains is only a speechless pain to which even bitterness is denied....Oh my God, what judgment has been loosed upon me. Tell me that I must still have the strength to live and to do what is true. Tell me that I am not mad. A stony darkness has crashed in. Oh, my friend, how small and unhappy I have become.

Fervently I embrace you....

(To Ludwig von Ficker in Innsbruck.)

The terrible things of the past days refer to his sister Grete's situation, according to Ficker, who also observed that Trakl kept the reasons for his tormented letter an absolute secret. Everything is circumstantial, though other communications provide a few clues. On July 7, 1912, Grete had married the much-older Arthur Langen, a Berliner of meager financial means who may have been a journalist or employed in a book establishment. The marriage may have followed on the heels of an affair with Buschbeck. In Berlin, Grete was drawn into a bohemian circle of productive literati through her husband, but her life with him has been pictured as unhappy. Almost a year later, Trakl wrote to Buschbeck in Salzburg and asked him if he knew whether or not Grete was visiting there; Buschbeck replied with an apology for a long-delayed response, but said that he had not seen Trakl's sister "here" in Innsbruck. Then, on August 15, 1913, a brief postcard by Trakl (referred to earlier) mentioned his impending trip to Venice. From that date on, the long-standing correspondence between the two ceased entirely. And so it was likely that some hint of Buschbeck's earlier affair reached Georg; he guessed at Grete's visit to Salzburg in 1913, and finally he received the news in the fall that Grete was pregnant. Like one betrayal after another, everything combined to plunge Trakl into the despair mirrored in his letter to Ficker. Yet, beneath this seething surface, his creative powers and writings perceptibly sharpened, the flow of his poetry remained unimpeded, and he gained a maturity of poetic form.

Innsbruck, December 13, 1913

Most esteemed Herr Kraus!
In these days of ravening drunkenness and criminal melancholy some verses have materialized, which I ask you to accept as a token of admiration for a man whose likeness is nowhere to be found in this world....Oh, also greet the magnificent Loos-Lucifer....
(To Karl Kraus in Innsbruck.)

Of pure lyrical breath was the poem "Ein Winterabend" that arose from the delirium described; its final form is found in "Winternacht"* ("Winter Night"), among the several poems dedicated to Kraus. Among Trakl's friends and acquaintances, only Kraus, Loos, Kokoschka, and Else Lasker-Schüler (a poet he was to meet later) possessed fine-honed intellectual creativity. With tribute to Trakl's uniqueness and with psychological perception, Kraus wrote in the journal he published, *Die Fackel*, that Trakl was one of those precocious and fully-matured beings who came into a world that gave them the "first and last feeling of wanting at once to return to the mother's womb." A number of Trakl's friends, including the dilettante poet Robert Müller, had gone to great lengths to include Trakl in plans for an anthology by young Viennese writers, but Trakl withdrew his contributions ostensibly on Kraus' advice. With fury, Müller wrote to Buschbeck about Trakl, "How can anyone have so little backbone to let himself be commanded by the hunchback Jew Kraus? ...a cripple in body and soul." Müller had earlier diagnosed Trakl as a sympathetic person and unhealthy "not for organic reasons but through slovenliness." Kraus, however, had better insight into Trakl's personality and greater ambitions for his career and recognition.

Innsbruck, possibly the beginning of January, 1914

...Things are not going well for me. Lost between moodiness and drunkenness, I lack strength and inclination to change a situation that daily appears more incurable. All that remains is a wish that a thunderstorm would overwhelm me and either cleanse or destroy me. O God, through what guilt and darkness must we go, after all. May we ultimately not succumb....
(To Karl Borromaeus Heinrich probably in Paris.)

In Trakl's letters are insistent suggestions that he felt vertiginous madness to have roots in organic rather than mental conditions. At a dinner party given by Ficker in January 1914, Trakl brusquely defended this view by citing Nietzsche's and Maupassant's final descent into madness. Ficker and his guests—the philosopher Carl Dallago and the Swiss writer Hans Limbach who recorded the conversations—were shocked and thought that in Trakl's ashen face "the demon of falsehood seemed to sparkle in his eyes." He went on to other self-identifications by saying that Tolstoy was "a Pan who broke down under the cross." Pressed by the guests, who were all part of the non-theological Christian Brenner circle, to give some indication of where he stood, Trakl declared that he was a Christian (not Christ as mistranslated by one American critic) and a Protestant, who unlike God's son could not claim the right to withdraw from the hell of cities. "Never has mankind," said Trakl, "sunk as deep as now, after the appearance of Christ," although, he continued, even those of other religious persuasions like the Buddhists have received the light from Christ. Biblical matters held little interest for Trakl except when they enlightened his own life-experiences and thoughts: "It is incredible how Christ with every simple word completely solves the deepest questions of mankind! Can one more completely solve the question of the communal bond between man and woman than through the commandment *They shall be as one flesh*?" Vehemently, Trakl went on to say, "One ought to strike dead those dogs who claim that woman only seeks sensual satisfaction! Woman, like each one of us, seeks only what is her due." Although he was referring to Dostoevsky's Sonya, it is the haunting figure of Grete in Trakl's biography, letters, and poetry—and her real or imagined betrayal of that communal sibling-bond—who comes alive in these assertions; they also harbor androgynous imagery. Brenner-circle doctrines permissively condoned the artist's search for self in the dark areas of being; articles and poems in the periodical often assumed a quasi-sensual tone and philosophical religiosity.

Events depicted in letters that follow again brutally connect the fates of the Trakl siblings. From March 15 to 24, 1914, Trakl spends troubled days with his sister in Berlin.

Berlin, Wilmersdorf, March 19, 1914

Several days ago, my sister had a miscarriage which was accompanied by extraordinarily vehement bleeding. Her condition is so very worrisome, all the more so because she has not taken nourishment for five days, that for the time being there is no thought of

her coming back to Innsbruck....
(To Karl Borromaeus Heinrich in Innsbruck.)

Berlin, Wilmersdorf, March 21, 1914

My poor sister is still suffering a great deal. Her life consists of heartrending sadness and at the same time of courageous bravery, so that once in a while I seem quite insignificant in the face of it. And, indeed, she deserves thousand times more than I to live in a circle of good and noble people, as it was granted me with over-abundance during difficult times.

I am thinking of staying in Berlin because during the entire day she is alone, and my presence is of some use....
(To Ludwig von Ficker in Innsbruck.)

During his brief stay in Berlin, Trakl met a number of contributors to the expessionistic periodical *Sturm*, with whom Grete and her husband associated. The former wife of *Sturm*'s publisher Herwarth Walden was the notable poet Else Lasker-Schüler. She wrote several poems about Trakl and told of their sparring "like playmates" about religion, which for her part reflected a devotion to Judaism and mystic visions of orientalism. As soon as he returned for brief shelter with Ficker, Trakl wrote his publisher Kurt Wolff that he wanted his manuscripts for his impending volume of poetry returned for revision and also to add "five poems which originated during my stay in Berlin...and which are dedicated to E. Lasker-Schüler," actually the second revision of a five-part poem, "Abendland"* ("Occident").

The months which follow are like a perverse scenario. A well-to-do schoolmate coldly turned down Trakl's request for a loan which would have helped Grete. In conversations during long excursions with the visionary poet Theodor Däubler, Trakl intensifies his monologues about death: "The manner of death is immaterial; death is so frightful—a step and fall—because ...we plunge into an incomprehensible blackness. How can dying—the seconds before eternity—be short?" His darkening mood is captured in a play fragment and a group of poems. Letters speak of plans to emigrate. In the midst of all this, Ficker gains a substantial and anonymous gift of money from Ludwig Wittgenstein that would have kept Trakl solvent for years if the historic assassination at Sarajevo had not occurred, triggering World War I. In August, Austria declares war against Serbia and breaks relations with Russia, a month before the war breaks out. As a lieutenant in the Innsbruck brigade of the army medical corps, Trakl on the eve of August 24/25 boards a "cattle" transport. Friends who saw him off retained a photo of him with a red carnation in his cap. The volunteer seemed relaxed and almost gay, as if burdens had been lifted, as he disappeared from his friends' sight; yet the apocalyptic finale and downturn in Trakl's life was about to ensue.

Ficker began receiving postcards and communications during Trakl's first days in the military inquiring about the works that had been in-press, including Trakl's requests for revisions. He writes of a good train trip on the way to Poland, "extraordinarily beautiful."

Galicia (Poland), beginning September, 1914

Dear Mama!
Heartiest greetings. Things go well with me. For weeks we have been criss-crossing Galicia and have not had anything to do as yet....
    With best greetings to you all.
                          Your Georg
(To Maria Trakl in Salzburg.)

Limanowa (West Galicia), beginning October, 1914

We now have four weeks of the most strenuous marches through all of Galicia behind us. For two days we rested in a small West Galician city amid soft and rolling hills, and we allowed ourselves a sense of peaceful well-being after the most recent events. Tomorrow or the day after, we will continue our march. A great new battle seems to be in the making. Would that heaven be favorable to us this time....
(To Ludwig von Ficker in Innsbruck.)

He sent a similar card to Adolf Loos, in which he told of being happy at the impending march into Russia, but otherwise being completely depressed with sadness. Trakl anticipated the battle that was to be renewed October 6-11 at Gródek/Rowa-Ruska in the Carpathians. It soon turned out to be a bloody experience that would also infuse his last poems. Ernst Günther Bleisch's *Georg Trakl* reconstructs the scene as it affected Trakl: The battle front had collapsed. The badly maimed, wounded, and mentally deranged streamed back in confusion and chaos. Trakl had been left in a barn to attend to ninety young and heavily-wounded soldiers. He was without sufficient medical supplies to alleviate their boundless suffering. The air stank with blood and pus and carbolic acid. Feverish, wax-yellow faces stared at Trakl and, amid wild cries of pain, many of the soldiers were pleading to be shot and to be put out of their misery. One soldier's leg had been torn off; some soldiers put bullets through their heads, splattering the walls. Trakl loses strength and rushes out helplessly. Outside of the barn, he sees bodies dangling from oak trees. Several of the bodies represent natives who were thought to be spies or Russophiles; some committed suicide. Trakl raises a pistol against himself (either then or several days later according to Ficker) but is disarmed. Soon thereafter, he is brought to a garrison hospital in Cracow. There he is given a convict-type gown and put into a cell-like room in company with a rapidly failing alcohol addict. He fears court-martial and a death sentence because of "cowardice in the face of the enemy" and for dereliction of duty. Although he had never voiced opposition to the war, its horror and reality overwhelmed him.

Cracow, Poland, October 12, 1914

Five days now, I have been in the garrison hospital for observation of my mental condition. My health undoubtedly has been impaired, and quite often I fall into unspeakable sadness. I hope that these days of depression will soon be over....
(To Ludwig von Ficker in Innsbruck.)

Ficker compassionately visited Trakl at the hospital from October 24 to 25. From there, both sent out greetings and communiques to friends; Ficker expected Trakl's imminent release. It may be that Ficker ignored the danger signals in evidence, because he was well acquainted with Trakl's ingrained pessimism through the years of their friendship. Trakl read to Ficker the recently composed poems "Klage"* ("Lament") and "Grodek,"* his descent into hell, and also the poem "Bussgedanken" by the German baroque poet Johann Christian Günther. One line of the poem of penance reads, "Oft ist ein guter Tod der beste Lebenslauf"; "A good death oft is the best life-course." Trakl then commented that Günther's verses were the most bitter ever penned by a German poet. (They were, and they expressed the pathos of a shattered life.

Günther radicalized poetic language in his time much as did Trakl later). Günther was about the same age as Trakl when he committed suicide in 1723. Ficker returned home, believing that Trakl was no worse mentally than anytime before.

Cracow, October 25, 1914

it would give me the greatest joy, if you would send me an advance copy of my new book sebastian im traum. am ill and in the cracow garrison hospital=georg trakl.
(Telegram to his publisher Kurt Wolff in Leipzig.)

Cracow, October 27, 1914

Dear, esteemed friend!
Enclosed are copies of the two poems I had promised. Since your visit to the hospital, I have been doubly sad. I feel myself almost as being past this world.

Finally, I want to add that in the event of my demise, it is my wish and will that my dear sister Grete is to own all that I have monetarily and to own other objects.... I embrace you deeply, dear friend.
(To Ludwig von Ficker in Innsbruck.)

Trakl's last poems "Klage"* ("Lament") and "Grodek"* were enclosed. In "Lament," the dark eagles of sleep and death swoop about the poet's head while the sister—of stormy melancholy—watches his decline.

Cracow, October 27, 1914

Enclosed are the revisions of the poem "Menschliches Elend" ("Human Misery") in my first book [*Gedichte*] and a revision of the poem "Traum des Bösen" ("The Evil One's Dream")....
(To Ludwig von Ficker in Innsbruck.)

This is thought to be Trakl's last letter. He changed one poem's title to "Menschliche Trauer" ("Human Sorrow"). As with other revisions of poems, he reshaped, replaced, or discarded old lines to suit a present moment. With scenes of the war still fresh in his mind, he created powerful new images:

It seems one hears the screams of bats,
In the garden, a grave being put together.
Through crumbled walls bones shimmer
And darkly a madman staggers past.

In the poem "Traum des Bösen," he replaced a descriptive line about "the fading away of a brown-gold gong's sounds" with a line that signalled and sealed his own fate: "the fading away of a death-bell's sounds." A return to first poems and converting them into his last symbolized for him the closing of a cycle of life filled with anguish.

Another strange return to the past was noted by Otto Basil: "It is striking that Trakl wrote the entire poem 'Klage' and the first six lines of 'Grodek' (in pencil) in the Latin script of his younger years rather than the more difficult-to-read cursive writing, perhaps intending to avoid any unpleasantness with the military censorship group who often were non-Germans."

The official medical dossier of Trakl at the Cracow garrison hospital reports matters clinically: Medical staffer Georg Trakl was under treatment here for mental disturbance (dementia praecox) and attempted suicide on the evening of November 2, 1914 through cocaine poisoning (drugs which he probably obtained at the field pharmacy where he was active earlier and which he hid despite our careful search). Despite all medical aid, he could not be saved. He died November 3 at 9 p.m. and was buried hereabouts at the Rakovicz cemetery.

Postscript

After Trakl's death, one finds poignant notes in correspondences about him. During his last days at the hospital, Mathias Roth, a young military orderly who was a mine worker in civilian life, attended to Trakl's needs and finally stood at his graveside. The young man's account bears an uncanny affinity to scenes in Tolstoy's *Death of Ivan Illych*, a story in which the peasant-servant is the only human to give unselfish comfort to his dying master. Roth has been harrassed by patients in the hospital, but Trakl treated him with a kindness that was immediately reciprocated by Roth with loyalty and affection. Roth wrote to Ficker on November 16, 1914, and a few lines from the untutored letter give much evidence of human concern:

...My superior [Trakl] always stood up for me personally and that I will never forget in my lifetime....And one thing which makes me happy is that you, dear sir, did see your best friend; I do not wish to be with these people here anymore.

Always and always I think about my dear, good superior, and that he had to meet his end in so pitiful a way?...He still was well in the evening and heartily told me at 6:30 to bring him black coffee in the morning, and that I should go to bed. The next morning it was different and my dear gentleman did not need black coffee anymore because during the night the dear God had taken him.

Although Grete was physically and emotionally shattered by the news of her brother's death, she expressed two wishes: to bring Georg's body back to home soil and to speak personally to the young orderly Roth. Grete was capable of writing only a few immediate lines to Ficker:

Esteemed Sir,
Most terrible is the death of my brother. God grant me soon the release for which I long. God bless you.
Your devoted G. L[angen].
(From Berlin, November 19, 1914)

Grete did visit with the Ficker family in Innsbruck, but three years later, almost to the day Ficker received her note, Grete absented herself during a party in Berlin and ended her life with a pistol shot. Trakl's bones were finally interred in 1925 at Mühlau-Innsbruck, the Tyrolian countryside he had often praised, and Ficker paid the poet tribute under a "transformed autumn sky."

APPENDIX

Translations by
James Wright

DE PROFUNDIS

It is a stubble field, where a black rain is falling.
It is a brown tree, that stands alone.
It is a hissing wind, that encircles empty houses.
How melancholy the evening is.

Beyond the village,
The soft orphan garners the sparse ears of corn.
Her eyes graze, round and golden, in the twilight
And her womb awaits the heavenly bridegroom.

On the way home
The shepherd found the sweet body
Decayed in a bush of thorns.

I am a shadow far from darkening villages.
I drank the silence of God
Out of the stream in the trees.

Cold metal walks on my forehead.
Spiders search for my heart.
It is a light that goes out in my mouth.

At night, I found myself in a pasture,
Covered with rubbish and the dust of stars.
In a hazel thicket
Angels of crystal rang out once more.

TRUMPETS

Under the trimmed willows, where brown children are playing
And leaves tumbling, the trumpets blow. A quaking of cemeteries.
Banners of scarlet rattle through a sadness of maple trees,
Riders along rye-fields, empty mills.

Or shepherds sing during the night, and stags step delicately
Into the circle of their fire, the grove's sorrow immensely old,
Dancing, they loom up from one black wall;
Banners of scarlet, laughter, insanity, trumpets.

THE RATS

In the farmyard the white moon of autumn shines.
Fantastic shadows fall from the eaves of the roof.
A silence is living in the empty windows;
Now from it the rats emerge softly

And skitter here and there, squeaking.
And a gray malodorous mist from the latrine
Follows behind them, sniffing:
Through the mist the ghostly moonlight quivers.

And the rats squeak eagerly as if insane
And go out to fill houses and barns
Which are filled full of fruit and grain.
Icy winds quarrel in the darkness.

A WINTER NIGHT

It has been snowing. Past midnight, drunk on purple wine, you leave the gloomy shelters of men, and the red fire of their fireplaces. Oh the darkness of night.

Black frost. The ground is hard, the air has a bitter taste. Your stars make unlucky figures.

With a stiff walk, you tramp along the railroad embankment with huge eyes, like a soldier charging a dark machinegun nest. Onward!

Bitter snow and moon.

A red wolf, that an angel is strangling. Your trouser legs rustle, as you walk, like blue ice, and a smile full of suffering and pride pertrifies your face, and your forehead is white before the ripe desire of the frost;

or else it bends down silently over the doze of the nightwatchman, slumped down in his wooden shack.

Frost and smoke. A white shirt of stars burns on your clothed shoulders, and the hawk of God strips flesh out of your hard heart.

Oh the stony hill. The cool body, forgotten and silent, is melting away in the silver snow.

Sleep is black. For a long time the ear follows the motion of the stars deep down in the ice.

When you woke, the churchbells were ringing in the town. Out of the door in the east the rose-colored day walked with silver light.

SLEEP

Not your dark poisons again,
White sleep!
This fantastically strange garden
Of trees in deepening twilight
Fills up with serpents, nightmoths,
Spiders, bats.
Approaching the stranger! Your abandoned shadow
In the red of evening
Is a dark pirate ship
On the salty oceans of confusion.
White birds from the outskirts of the night
Flutter out over the shuddering cities
Of steel.

SELECT BIBLIOGRAPHY
OF SECONDARY SOURCES IN ENGLISH

Bance, Alan Frederick. "The Kaspar Hauser Legend and Its Literary Survival." *German Life and Letters*, NS 28 (1974/75), pp. 199-210.

Detsch, Richard. *Symbolon: The Union of Opposites in Georg Trakl's Poetry*. University Park: Penn State Press, 1983.

Hamburger, Michael. "Georg Trakl." *Reason and Energy: Studies in German Literature*. New York: Grove, 1957, pp. 239-272.

Harries, Karsten. "Language and Silence: Heidegger's Dialogue with Georg Trakl." *Boundary II*, Vol. IV, No. 2 (Winter, 1976), pp. 495-511.

Heidegger, Martin. "Language in the Poem. A Discussion on Georg Trakl's Poetic Work." *On The Way to Language*. Tr. Peter D. Herz. New York: Harper & Row, 1982.

Kurrik, Maire. *Georg Trakl*. Columbia Essays on Modern Writers, 72. New York: Columbia University Press, 1974.

Lindenberger, Herbert. "Georg Trakl and Rimbaud: A Study in Influence and Development." *Comparative Literature*, 10 (1958), pp. 21-35.

————. *Georg Trakl*. New York: Twayne, 1971.

Neumann, Eric. "Georg Trakl: The Person and the Myth." *Creative Man: Five Essays*. Tr. Eugene Rolfe. Princeton: Princeton University Press, 1980.

Sharp, Francis Michael. *The Poet's Madness: A Reading of Georg Trakl*. Ithaca: Cornell University Press, 1981.

ACKNOWLEDGEMENTS

1. Die Rechte fur das Werk Georg Trakls liegen beim Otto Müller Verlag, Salzburg, die Texte dieser Ausgabe wurden dem Werk "Dichtungen und Briefe," Salzburg, 1969, entnommen.

2. Most of the poems in translation in this volume first appeared in *Georg Trakl: Selected Poems*, edited by Christopher Middleton and published by Jonathan Cape, Ltd. in London (1968). Grateful acknowledgement is extended to the Georg Trakl Estate, to Jonathan Cape Ltd., and to the translators and editor for permission to reprint translations by Robert Grenier and David Luke.

3. All translations by Michael Hamburger reprinted with Michael Hamburger's permission. The selections included herein but not collected in the above-mentioned *Selected Poems* were first published as follows: "Dejection" in *Stand* and in *The Penguin Book of First World War Poetry*; "Music in the Mirabel" in *Adam*.

4. All translations by Christopher Middleton reprinted with Christopher Middleton's permission.

5. "Trumpets," "De Profundis," "The Rats," "A Winter Night," and "Sleep" in James Wright's translation all copyright © 1971 by James Wright, and reprinted from James Wright's *Collected Poems* by permission of Wesleyan University Press and Edith Anne Wright.

6. "Caspar Hauser Song," "South Wind," and "The Soul's Springtime" in David Luke's translation are reprinted with David Luke's permission.

Library of Congress Cataloging in Publication Data
Main entry under title:

Georg Trakl, a profile.

   Bibliography: p.
   I. Trakl, Georg, 1887-1914.   II. Graziano, Frank,
1955-   .
PT2642.R22A2 1983   831'.912   83-13644
ISBN 0-937406-28-7
ISBN 0-937406-27-9 (pbk.)
ISBN 0-937406-29-5 (lim. ed.)